Startup Musician

By Brandon Shaw

Edited by Allison Shaw

Cover Illustration & Design by Creative Seven

Photos by Ace Barro

ISBN-10: 1535278846
ISBN-13: 978-1535278843

For Faith

My partner, best friend, baby mama, pard'ner, green-lighter of my crazy ideas, best thing, and wife.

TABLE OF CONTENTS

STARTUP MUSICIAN

MAKE MONEY MAKING MUSIC

by

BRANDON SHAW

CHAPTER 1
I HAVE A MUSIC DEGREE. NOW WHAT?

How Did I Get Here?

I grew up in a music-filled home. My mom plays the piano. My grandma plays the piano. My great grandma was my mom's piano teacher and so on down the line. I started playing the piano at age five because that's what my family does. For me, it wasn't a conscious decision to start playing music; it was just something that everyone I knew did. Music was as present in my early life as Lego® or Disney's *DuckTales* (A-whoo-oo!).

At age 10 I picked up the electric bass because my older brother Kendon played guitar and his band needed a bass player. I didn't make this decision by weighing the options and deciding which instrument to play. My brother needed a bass player, so I played the electric bass. I picked up the upright base around the same time.

I played the bass throughout junior high and high school in pretty much every ensemble imaginable: jazz band, concert band, jazz choir, concert choir, string orchestra, symphony orchestra. I also played in church bands and in my own rock band with friends, Leonard's Moped

Bass playing baby Brandon circa 1997.

When I got to college, majoring in music was a no brainer. After all, it's just *what I did*. I didn't bother with sports, or debate team, or any other extracurricular clubs. I didn't have time with all of that music going on. I attended a four-year university and earned a bachelor of arts in music for bass performance.

Shortly after graduation, shiny new degree in hand, I had a wake up call; life is expensive. My landlord expected a rent check *every single month*. As did AT&T and the company that insured my beat up Volvo station wagon. I also had to buy gas for my Volvo station wagon and pay for constant repairs for my Volvo station wagon. (You don't technically *need* a working speedometer, right?)

Looking at my non-music-major friends, something didn't add up. During college, I was the one who took the maximum number of units allowed, and then some! In order to fulfill scholarship requirements and graduate in four years, I played in several ensembles for exactly zero credit. My business major friends finished for the day at 4 p.m., just as I was going into my evening block of rehearsals. As a music major I put in significantly more time, and yet, after graduation, the business majors went on to get full-time jobs that paid good money while I was sitting at home panicking about my station wagon. (It's not a *huge* deal if the gas pedal sticks to the floor, right?) And that's when it me; my new degree, my entire education, all of those extra ensembles I played in, and all of the hours I logged in the practice room had done exactly one thing, made me a good musician.

Now What?

Being a good musician is definitely a good thing. Art has value. I believe in music and the power it has to move people. But in the process of becoming a good musician, the hours and hours of practicing, rehearsing, and devoting my life to this craft, I had failed to ask one crucial question. How do I turn this into my job? How do I make a living as a professional musician? I had spent so much time pursuing music because it was just what I did that I never stopped to think about how I would make a living out of it. I just figured it would all work out somehow.

On top of that, I spent so much time developing my musicianship that I literally had no other viable skills. Music was, and still is, the only thing I'm really good at. I say this not to brag about my ability as a musician, but to illustrate my inability to do just about *anything* else.

Add to that the fact that, I don't write original music. I tried to write a song when I was thirteen and it was terrible. I tried to rhyme "home" with "gnome." My family still makes fun of me. This made it even more difficult to imagine what I should be doing as a musician. Do I join a band as the bass player? Do I have to get really good at slap bass? How is this supposed to work?

No Fortune 500 company was going to hire me to play bass full time (I still can't believe no one would go for that.), and I was out of the running for a serious orchestra seat. I was a good musician, but had no idea how to earn a living.

With no clear goal in mind I decided to continue playing music (because, as you may recall, I didn't know how to do much else) and to my surprise I discovered an entirely new world. It's a world full of great people who make an actual living doing what they love. At first it's not all that obvious, but when you know where to look, you'll start seeing them all over the place; they are freelance musicians.

There are a few things you should know up front about being a freelance musician. First, it's a lot of work. Yes, you're doing something that you love, and that's a hell of a lot better than crunching numbers in a cubicle (I would imagine), but there's still *a lot of work* that goes into it. You have to be really excellent at something and continually work to get better.

Second, there are a lot of different ways to make a living in music. There is no one "right" way. It all depends on what you're good at, what you like, and what other people value.

You're going to get bits and pieces of my story throughout this book, but for now I'll skip to the conclusion and tell you that I make my living as a professional musician. It hasn't always been easy but I can't imagine doing anything else.

And Then I Wrote A Book

Over the decade I've spent building my career I've browsed through bookstores in search of a book about being a freelance musician, a book that "gets me," and what I'm trying to do. But I've never found it. Books with titles like *Marketing for Musicians in the Net Age* or *How to Make it Big in the Post-Napster Era* are full of advice that is not only dated (Net Age? Really? Are we in the classic Sandra Bullock 90s tech-action-adventure movie *The Net?*), but also tend to come from older musicians. I believe that older people are wise and we have *lots* to learn from them, but at the same time, the music business that they came up in is *not* the same business we're in today.

Books about royalties, recording contracts, copyright law, unions, and how to get your band out there have been on the shelves for years, but they just don't apply to someone working to make it as a freelance musician. And let's face it, they're either stale, a bit boring, or trying way too hard to sell books to young people (by using words like "Net Age"). So I wrote this book. I wanted to put together a resource that has practical steps you can take to build a solid music career.

While it's impossible to give you an exact road map of how to build a career as a freelance musician because the road is a little different for everyone, I can give you pretty much everything I've learned on my own journey as a freelance musician.

This book also contains interviews with 10 professional musicians living very different lives and doing a wide variety of things with their careers. You'll get a snapshot into their lives, their work, and some specific "how to" advice, like how to get more students, how to get a composition gig out of nowhere, and how to juggle a family and a music career (*and you'll find out if it's possible to play trombone for a living*).

From this, you will have to forge your own path. It's a little different for everyone, but the concepts are universal.

Who This Book Is For

- If you're a good musician who doesn't know what to do next, this book is for you.

- If you have a college degree, it's for you.

- If you *don't* have a college degree, it's also for you.

- If you're trying to start a career as a freelance musician, this is for you.

- If you're trying to grow your music career, it's for you as well.

- If you're a musician who doesn't write or play your own original music, this book is *especially* for you.

Who This Book Is Not For

- If you're in a band and you're hoping to make it big, get signed, sell a million records, and tour the world playing your songs, this book is not for you! There are plenty of other books for that. This book is focused on building your career as a *freelance* musician.

- If you're *kind of a douchebag*, this book is not for you. If there's one thing I do not tolerate, it's douchebaggery. If this is you, put down this book, grab your indoor sunglasses, and crank up the Nickelback. See you down at the lake, bro!

• If you're not willing to work, log the long hours, learn new things, and continually get up after you fail, this book is not for you. Doing the freelance thing means that you're starting a business, and as any business owner will tell you, *it's a lot of work.*

"I can only show you the door. You're the one that has to walk through it."

~ Jesus, or Morpheus from *The Matrix*, I can't remember.

Regardless of who said it, this quote is directly applicable here. In the pages that follow you'll learn a lot about how to become a freelance musician and what to expect along the way. You'll hear directly from musicians already making a living as freelancers, and you'll brainstorm ideas for your own career. But then it's up to you to apply this stuff, to figure out what your version of this looks like, and to continue to push yourself as a musician and entrepreneur.

Ready?

CHAPTER 2
WHAT IS A STARTUP MUSICIAN?

Will There Be A Blood Oath?

I grew up playing music all through elementary, middle, and high school. I did all of the things you would expect; I took lessons and played in school groups, at church, and with my own original band. I like to think I had good taste in music, at least better than my non-music friends. After all, I was a *musician*. I understood stuff.

But any time someone found out that I played the bass, the first question they would ask me was, "Who are some of your favorite bass players?" This seems like an easy enough question to answer. After all, I was a *musician*, right? I knew stuff. My typical answer started with me shrugging awkwardly, looking at my shoes, and then muttering, "The bass player in Coldplay?"

"I'm blanking on his name...uh...Tom...Coldplay?"

I didn't know anything about freelance musicians back then. At the time, my knowledge of musicians was limited to the concept of BANDS. That's BANDS with a capital B, as well as a capital A, N, D, and S. Let me explain.

When I was in high school I had this idea that a band was like an unbreakable bond. (You may have had the same idea.) If you were in a band, you took a metaphorical (or sometimes literal) blood oath. You had each other's back for better or worse. You all slept in the band van, played shows, split the money four ways, and were dead set on getting a record deal. This is the rock star dream. It was you and your band versus the world. Oh, and if you were in a band, and you left that band to join another band, man, that was unforgivable.

"With this blood oath, I hereby swear that we are a band now and forever. Now that that's over, my mom made brownies. You guys want some?"

It's about the passion, man! It's about the music! It's about playing sold out shows night after night, selling a million records, partying hard after every show, groupies, getting wasted, and living like there's no tomorrow. This ultimate rock star dream may be the reason so many music legends die at the age of twenty-seven.

This concept of the BAND and living the rock star lifestyle is how many people (including your extended family) still perceive today's music industry. (Don't worry Aunt Linda; I would *never* bite the head off a dove.) The problem is, that stereotype is about as accurate for professional musicians as *CSI: Miami* is for police detectives.

"He came here to play guitar, but it looks like somebody played him."

Sure, it's a fun show to watch, and David Caruso delivers some of the cheesiest one-liners on TV, ("She came to Miami to catch some sun, but it looks like *something* caught her!" *Seriously?*), but it's not an accurate picture of the day-to-day work of actual police detectives. Just ask a police officer, or detective, or the relative of a police officer, or someone who knows a police officer, or pretty much anyone else you can think of. The same is true of musicians.

Are there musicians out there living the rock star life? Of course. But the Internet, musical progress, and time itself have opened the door for a different type of musician; the one who wants to do great work but then go home to their family at the end of the night.

I call this person a Startup Musician.

The Startup Musician

A Startup Musician is not a core member of a band, like the bass player in Coldplay (whatever that guy's name is). A Startup Musician isn't a tenured member of a large orchestra (which is it's own entirely different world), and they aren't trying to "make it big" as a rock star.

A Startup Musician is involved with many different artists, bands, and groups. They play different music in different places with different people all the time. It's not breaking the blood oath; it's part of the job. They most likely do multiple things under the umbrella of music. Maybe they play or perform, but also teach. Maybe they teach, but also do audio engineering. Maybe it's composition and the occasional tour with a high-profile artist. Whatever the combo, they're almost always doing more than one thing. But perhaps most importantly, they want to live a relatively normal life. No groupies, no crazy all night benders, no biting heads off poultry. This isn't the 1960s.

A typical Startup Musician is not a household name. Your Aunt Linda has no idea who they are. She may have heard them play or seen them on TV, but she's not going to have the same reaction as hearing you talk about Rod Steward. (Oh honey, he's just so great! He's coming to the Muckleshoot Casino in June; we just *have* to go!)

When it comes to startups, we're most familiar with the tech world: the Facebooks, the AirBnBs, and the Instagrams. Sure, they're famous now, but when they launched, their founders didn't *really* know what they were yet. They had some great ideas, but they didn't have it nailed down out of the gate.

A college student makes a website where students at his school can have their own page to write comments, share a photo, and "poke" each other (I still don't really understand the sentiment behind this.) It expands to any student at any college and ultimately to anyone in the world. And then it wasn't just status updates. It was photos, videos, links, games, messaging, and marketplaces. As of this writing, Facebook has 700 million active users and is valued at $483 billion[1].

Dropbox™ was founded in 2007 and launched its service in 2008. Co-founder Drew Houston was constantly losing his USB drive and wanted to build a better solution. By 2014 the file-hosting service was valued at $10 billion and by the second quarter of 2015 had over 300 million users in more than 200 counties[2]. Take a second to soak that in. That's $10,000,000,000, as in a 10 with nine more zeroes.

Before Dropbox we stored papers in actual boxes.
This was before the Internet. It was a dark time.

---

[1] Eric Jackson. "How much would Facebook be worth if it hadn't bought Instagram?" Forbes. (April 30, 2017).

[2] Evan Tarver. "Startup Analysis: How Much is Dropbox Worth?" Investopedia. (August 20, 2015).

A coder made an app that included everything from check-ins, to status updates, to photos. It wasn't doing very well and the whole experience felt cluttered and confusing so the team threw everything out and started over. This time, they decided to focus on just one thing, photos. In April 2017, Instagram exceeded 700 million users[3] with 400 million using the service on a daily basis[4]. Even Pope Frances has 2.9 million followers[5].

When each of these startup companies launched, they weren't fully formed. Their founders didn't know exactly what they were going to be. They started with one thing, tried a bunch of different versions of that, and adapted to what their customers wanted.

Startup Musicians follow the same pattern. You've just earned a music degree, or decided to pursue your lifelong music dream. You're thinking, "Maybe I've really got something here!" Under the music umbrella, you probably have a few different skills. As you move forward, your task is to experiment with those skills, keep working, try new things, grow, learn, and pivot when needed. Eventually, it'll be very clear what you do best and what people actually want.

For me, one of my skills is the upright bass. I've played in orchestras since I was ten and in jazz bands since I was thirteen but today I don't play much classical and I'm not a serious "jazz cat." So what do I do with those skills? I get called for singer-songwriter, funky upright, acoustic, mellow,

---

[3] www.instagram.com. Accessed May 22, 2017.

[4] Gabriela Vatu. "Instagram has officially hit 400 million daily active users, which is a great feat considering the app's history." Softpedia. (February 2, 2017).

[5] Kathleen Chaykowski. "Instagram, The $50 Billion Grand Slam Driving Facebook's Future." Forbes. (August 23, 2016).

emotional music. The ability to play upright bass, while maintaining pop sensibilities is apparently a skill that people value. I'm never going to play in the LA Philharmonic, and I'm unlikely to sub for Christian McBride, but I am going to get called by an artist you may or may not have heard of to play live. And they'll probably sound a lot like Mumford & Sons.

But I also play electric bass, teach upright and electric bass, manage and write for *Startup Musician*, play for a local church, and perform with my beautiful, very talented wife.

Gone are the days of the rock star dream, "getting signed," and band blood oaths. We're living in a new era.

As a freelance musician, you will be in charge of your own career. You will be running your own startup. Just because you aren't playing the Staples Center doesn't mean you have to eat Top Ramen® every day. You're a good musician. Now let's start your business. You are now running your own startup.

You are a Startup Musician.

CHAPTER 3
DRUMS & WHALE CALLS
W/BRYAN TAYLOR

Photo: Kaitlin Gladney

If you listen to the *Startup Musician* podcast, you're probably familiar with Bryan Taylor. He's the guest in episode four, and he's actually the only *double* guest. Let me explain.

We sat down and recorded a podcast interview. He had loads of good stuff to say, and plenty of jokes. The content was great! But my old MacBook had a hard time handling the interview. I placed the computer right by the microphone to record Bryan and when the fan kicked in to cool down my aging laptop, the loud whirring drowned him out. Obviously I discovered this much too late and the interview was completely unusable. Lucky for me, Bryan is the kind of guy who says, "Yes, absolutely" when you say, "Hey, tech fail, can we re-record the entire thing?"

Bryan is one of the most musical drummers I've ever had the pleasure of playing with. Not only that, he's one of my favorite people on the planet. As we sat down for what would now be our *third* interview, I wanted to get into the nitty-gritty of what Bryan does, how he does it, and how he balances his life.

# # #

What kinds of things make up your job?

Collectively my job would be drums and percussion, playing for different artists and recordings. I also do some programming and drums and tracks, and then I also play guitar and sing. So sometimes that comes up as well.

What falls under the umbrella of "drums"?

For in-town stuff, I play with singer-songwriters, different churches, recordings for different artists, help with producing. I also play for some TV stuff when it comes up, which is nice. I have done commercials. And then I do touring as well with different artists, most recently with a guy named Eric Hutchinson and another guy named Tommy Walker.

What is one thing you are particularly good at?

I do feel like I've played a lot of different styles over time. Depending on what I'm doing, I feel like I can be creative with different people using all of the different styles and things that I've learned. I studied jazz in college and even after college I played it a lot, so if I'm doing a singer-songwriter thing, or working in the studio, I feel like there are jazz elements that I can bring in, or Broadway show tunes, and rock and pop and all kinds of stuff like that.

I also do percussion stuff so I can add that onto the drum set and be creative, whether it's playing with my hands or hot rods or trying to get different sounds going. So that creative range, I feel like, maybe that's my one thing.

Bryan is an incredibly humble person, so I'll say what he's not saying; Bryan is great at incorporating many styles of music into his playing, and bringing to the music things you would never imagine. He's perfectly comfortable just playing groove, but when the situation calls for it, he'll switch to playing the drum set with his hands, or playing a glass of water, or getting out from behind the drums, walking over to the acoustic guitar player, and playing percussion on the guitar itself. Bryan isn't bound by the traditional idea of what it means to be a drummer. He is always looking for new ways to make music.

Quick side story for you: Once I was playing jazz with Bryan. When it came time for a drum solo, he let loose. First he started with brushes, playing things that I'm still not sure how he played. Then he switched to his hands. As he did this, it was clear that the attention in the room was focused solely on him. As he continued to play crazy rhythms, banging away with his hands on the snare drum, I noticed an audience member on the side of the stage. He was staring at Bryan, mesmerized. As Bryan continued his solo, this guy didn't blink at all, he just stared. Near the end of his solo, Bryan put in a short break, licked his finger, and dragged it across the head of the rack tom. The resulting sound was similar to a whale call. At the moment, the mesmerized man let out a loud, "OH MY GOD!" as if he had just seen Michael Jordan sink a half-court swish. It was, and still is, one of my favorite memories of Bryan's playing.

What does an average week of work look like for you?

Monday is usually a day to get stuff done, an "off" day

from music. It doesn't have to be, but a lot of times it can be. Tuesday I try to make my "lessons" day. I teach at Citrus College in Glendora [California] and I usually go in and try to get all my students done in one day and try not to have to do make up lessons. I try to not schedule anything else that day.

Wednesdays can vary. Sometimes I'll have a rehearsal or a church might have a Wednesday night service or a midweek thing that I might go play for. Thursdays could be a rehearsal for somebody I'm playing for on Saturday.

Fridays I could be playing a pop gig or a cover band gig. Saturday is playing with the artist, and on Sundays, a lot of times, I'll be playing at a church in the morning and sometimes in the evening as well.

When you have a lot of activities that take place in the evening, how do you schedule your daytime hours?

I have a wife and a daughter and I am so excited about both of them. My role has kind of changed in the last year and a half or so, because she's a year and half old.

Bryan looks right into the camera and says jokingly: "If you're sixteen and thinking about having a kid and a musical career you might want to hold off on [the kid part] for just a little bit because at my age (*Bryan is in his early 30s*) I'm trying to figure out how to do the two and at sixteen, it's probably even harder.

Because my wife has a job, I do try to squeeze in my stuff at night and so I can take care of our daughter during the day. But we also hire a nanny to come in and watch her when I have things that I need to do during the day.

During the day I might be working on learning music. I'll sit down and chart out the different things for the week. If I need to program click or tracks or something, I can do that all from my house. I practice during the day and sometimes I'll have meetings. So the day can be more like prep for the things happening at night, which is nice, unless it's a recording thing; that's going to take all day.

What does your actual "work" look like (beyond playing the gig at night)?

If I get a list of songs from somebody that I need to learn, for me what works best is to scratch out my own rhythm chart that I know makes sense. I find that's an easier way for me to learn a song and get it under my fingers quicker. Sometimes it's sitting in Logic®[6] and creating the click tracks for things that I know we're going to need for the whole band to use. Or somebody will send me files and I'll drop them into Ableton Live™[7], put them together, and adjust the levels and things like that.

Then there's making sure you have the right gear for what you're going to be doing. So, I have to think through my week because I have different drum sets for different things. I have a storage unit and I have to make sure I can get all of the stuff that I need for that week out of the storage unit and make sure that I have my car traded out for what I have coming the next day.

Do you have any sort of regular schedule or routine?

I don't have a specific routine. A lot of times I'll take Sunday to look out at the week and say, "Okay, when am I going to be able to learn these songs for this thing if its coming up on this day?" I'll set a thing of saying, "On

---

[6] Logic is an application of Apple Inc.

[7] Live™ is the music-making software by Ableton. Startup Musician is an independent publication and has not been authorized, sponsored, or otherwise approved by Ableton AG. Live™ is a trademark of Ableton AG.

Wednesday I know I'm gonna have this time open to learn these songs." With the exception of Tuesdays when I'm doing lessons, my schedule can really vary from week to week depending on what's going on, where I need to be, and finding babysitting and things like that, which come with getting older and having a family.

Do you have any non-music hobbies?

I don't now if this counts as a hobby or not. But I *really* like documentaries. They're relaxing for me; I like learning about stuff.

Top three documentaries, Go!

I really like presidential documentaries. I love learning about the presidents. Number two, lately has been the murder documentaries. *Making a Murderer* is really good. I like *Dateline*. Give me a good 'ol "Whodunnit" any time. It's always the husband or the wife. And then number three has got to be music. I like music documentaries of course.

What is your life like? How do your wife and daughter fit into your career?

That's inappropriate. Next question. *Bryan laughs, and then proceeds to give his real answer.*

My wife is also a musician. She's a singer, a wonderful singer. We talked about music a lot before we got married because we were both doing the music thing and we both kind of knew that our life wasn't going to look a lot like our friends' lives. She's been gracious with me when I have needed to go out on the road for months at a time.

There was a point where I had a full-time job and she was doing music stuff and then we switched roles. She's now the dean of the music department at a private high school.

21

We always try take time on Sunday to look at the week coming up and say, "When am I gonna see you this week? Where are the pockets of time that were gonna run into each other?" We have dinner together. Our New Year's resolution was to have a date night once a week because with music stuff coming up its easy to blow past things and be like, "Oh I haven't had dinner with you in seven months," so it's nice to plan that kind of thing.

Now, having a daughter, that adds a whole different element to it. I think it's valuable to spend time with her, especially if I know I'm going to be going out on the road for a while. It's also important for me to cherish the time that I get to be home; find "Daddy" days to spend with her. I'm sure this is all so exciting for all of the young up and coming musicians to hear, "Find daddy days".

Bryan is a great musician. When you see him play live, it's clear that he absolutely loves playing music, but when he's around his family, it's clear that he loves them even more. Life as a freelance musician can be hard to balance with a family, but Bryan is setting a pretty good example for those up and comers.

You can make it all fit. Your spouse has to be very understanding, and you have to be willing to work together on it because it just looks completely different than the nine-to-five life that people do. It's not like musicians are the only people who are busy, but it's just weird timing. You could be gone for two months, it's strange, and it's even harder with a baby. Just because I'm out in front of people playing and doing all this stuff, that doesn't mean that what I want is more important than my wife's work. So taking that into account and saying, "This isn't just about me."

What is the hardest part about being a freelance musician?

At this point, it's the uncertainty of not knowing where

it's going sometimes. Each year of my life feels like a new adventure, but it's an adventure where you're not quite sure where you're going to end up. It's like you're waiting at the airport with your bags, but you're not sure which plane you're going to get on. So you're often asking, "What is the next step?"

You can take people's advice, you can practice really hard, but sometimes, you're taking a stab in the dark. You're connecting with people and you're hoping it's a good connection and then it may turn out to be nothing. With being older and having a family, I want to make sure that I am providing and contributing.

If you could play one show with one artist, dead or alive, who would it be?

I'm not *just* a jazz drummer, but if I could sit behind the drums and play with The Count Basie Orchestra with Frank Sinatra singing in front, I mean that's pretty awesome. As a big band drummer, it's like driving a party bus. That's what I feel being a big band drummer is.

Bryan is a great musician and a great person and although he may not know how his career will unfold in the future, because of these traits he'll do just fine.

CHAPTER 4
FINDING YOUR NICHE

The MVP

There's a term from the tech startup world that you need to know: MVP. This has nothing to do with sports and it doesn't mean that you're extra special (Sorry). MVP stands for "minimum viable product" and it references the most basic version of the product that a tech company is trying to build.

For example, Facebook's MVP looked nothing like the Facebook of today. When it launched in 2004, Facebook did one simple thing really well; it hosted profiles for students at Harvard that other Harvard students could comment on. That was it. It wasn't until 2005 that they opened up to other universities, and 2006 when they opened up to everyone 13 and over. Then came photos, and chat, and video, and FarmVille (Worst three years of my life!), and logging into other sites with your Facebook account. They are still constantly adding features.

In 2012 they added a universally unwanted feature: everyone's mom joined!

Or what about those two guys in San Francisco were so broke that they didn't have enough money to pay their rent, but they did have three air mattresses. They pieced together a website (really just a blog with a map on it) and offered to rent the air mattresses on their floor for an upcoming industry conference. Three people showed up and paid $80 each. This got them thinking, forget about their one apartment, what if everyone could rent out their own apartment from the website they made? Hello MVP! Lots of tweaks, changes, and room rentals later, AirBnB has more than 3,000,000 listings (including more than 1,500 castles) in over 191 countries[8] and is valued at $30 billion dollars[9].

"That'll be $30 billion dollars, thank you very much."

Almost every startup starts with something that is *good enough*, and focuses on doing that one thing really well. For Dropbox it was file syncing, for Instagram it was photos with cool filters, for Airbnb it was about renting rooms.

So how does this translate to you as a musician?

You don't need to do everything you've imagined to get started. In fact, you shouldn't even try. You don't need to play every style, know every lick, or even be the best *all around* player. You start by getting really good at one or two things.

"But I want to write, arrange, perform, produce, tour, score films, teach, and be a guitar luthier!" you say? Hey, I get

---

[8] www.airbnb.com. Accessed May 22, 2017.

[9] Matt Rosoff. "AirBnb is now worth $30 billion" Business Insider. (August 6, 2016).

it! I'm the same way. You can make doing multiple things your ultimate goal, but take it one thing at a time. Rome wasn't built in a day. Neither was Facebook, and neither will your music career.

Pick one or two things from your list and focus on doing those things exceptionally well. Become the best you possibly can. You can always add additional things later, but for now, you need an MVP. Focus on going deep with a few things instead of going shallow with everything. This concept is the foundation of building a successful tech startup, and it's also how you build a successful career as a Startup Musician.

Who Would You Call?

As a professional musician, you want to be the first person people call when they need a _____.
With that in mind, you may think you need to play everything. If you can play rock, punk, jazz, soul, fusion, classical, Latin, and Riverdance, then you'll get called for *all* of those gigs.

FALSE!

I'm here to tell you that that thinking is exactly backwards. If you want to be a successful musician, you actually need to focus on doing *less*. (Besides, the golden age of Riverdance is long gone.)

Like a phoenix from the ashes, I shall step dance my way out of obscurity.

I once received a business card from a musician that listed his name, two phone numbers, an email address, and the following description:

TEVIN SEBASTIAN
GUITAR, BASS, VOCALS, KEYS,
PRODUCING, SONGWRITING, LESSONS,
VIOLIN, ARRANGING, FILM SCORES...
YEAH, I DO IT ALL!

What do you think I did with that card?

- If you guessed, "Called him up for a gig," you are incorrect.

- If you guessed, "Framed it and put it on my wall as a reminder of what not to do," you are the winner!

The downside of the "doing everything" approach is that there's nothing *unique* about you. No one knows how to define the things that make you truly great. If you try to do everything, you'll get called for nothing.

Let's say you need a drummer to play on your acoustic singer-songwriter album. You think through drummers that you know and your options include:

- A drummer who boasts that he can play "any style, any tempo, any time signature." The YouTube videos of him playing complicated Latin-infused-neo-speed-trip-hobbit-core have over 100,000 views and he's been featured on gospelchops.com.

- A drummer who plays lots of acoustic gigs, has recorded with multiple singer-songwriter artists that you know, and has a unique custom dual-cajon setup with a tambourine kick pedal.

Who are you going to call? (If you said, "Ghostbusters," congratulations! That was the secret third option.

Here's another example: you're hungry and you want a cheeseburger. There are two restaurants right next to each other.

- McDonald's

- In-N-Out Burger

The correct choice is obviously In-N-Out (and I will fight any man who says otherwise). In-N-Out does one thing exceptionally well: burgers. They also make exceptional fries and shakes, but that's it! If you want a chicken sandwich, or a salad, or a Filet-o-Fish® (Why?), you're going to have to go to McDonald's.

Even though In-N-Out offers fewer things, the things that they *do* offer are so much better than the competition. It's a no-brainer. If you want lots of different types of mediocre food, you go to McDonald's. But when was the last time you said, "Oh man! Let's go to McDonald's!"? When you were five, that's when. And even then, it was only because you got a toy with your meal.

"But what about all of those untapped gigs?" you ask?

Resist! What I'm saying here may fly in the face of everything you've been taught. I too have wrestled with the "You need to be able to do everything, play any style authentically, be able to perfectly execute every style of music!" mindset. It comes with the territory.

In order to succeed as a Startup Musician, you *will* have to do multiple things. But please don't confuse "multiple things" with "all of the things." Maybe you play live gigs, but also teach, or you do lots of studio work and also have great chart making abilities. You will need a combination of skills to combat the inconsistency that comes with being a full-time musician; it's just part of the job. Sometimes you are so busy you forget to eat (December); other times you're barely scraping by (Hello January!).

Do multiple things, yes, but don't fall into the trap of thinking that you can or should do everything. There just aren't enough hours in the day to dedicate to getting *really* excellent at everything. You need to find the minimum viable product that you can deliver in order to get working. Your goal is to get *incredibly* good at just a few things. No one can do everything with complete mastery. No one.

Well, no one except James Franco.

Yes, you should absolutely study as many genres of music as you can (even Riverdance, if you're into that). Yes, you should practice different stuff. Yes, you need try multiple things. But you don't need to (and shouldn't try to) do everything.

I am *never* going to be called for an honest-to-God Latin gig. Ever. I never have and I never will. You know why? Because I'm just too white. Sure, I play some Latin stuff from time to time, but the subtleties that make that style authentic and feel really good just aren't there for me. And that's okay. I still play a lot of gigs, just not the Latin ones.

I would rather focus my time and energy on becoming

exceptional at the things I'm good at than trying to build up the things that just aren't me.

Play to Your Strengths

It's time to do some soul searching. I want you to write down the two or three main categories of Startup Musician work that you want to pursue. No more than three. Do you want to play and teach? Studio record and compose? Audio engineer and copy work? Pick your big categories and write them down.

Now, within those categories, I want you to write three or four (no more) sub-categories. Under "Live Gigs" maybe you'll put "singer-songwriter, soul/R&B, worship." Maybe under "Copy Work" you'll write, "basic rhythm charts and lead sheets," as opposed to "full orchestral movie scores." You get the idea, right?

Here's an example.

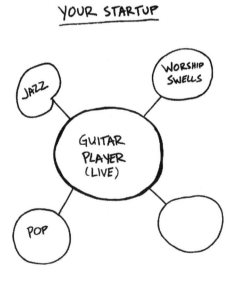

YOUR STARTUP

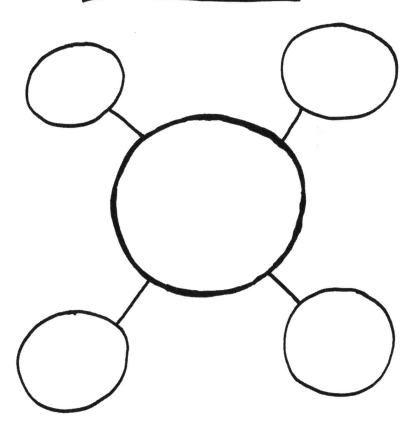

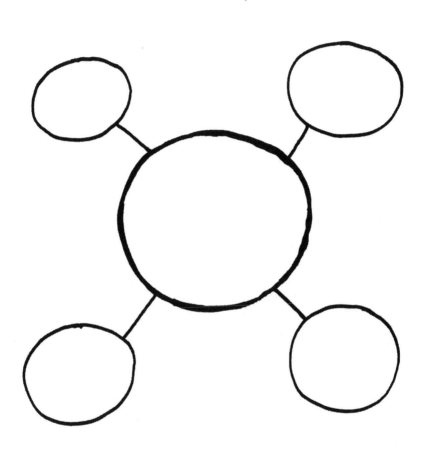

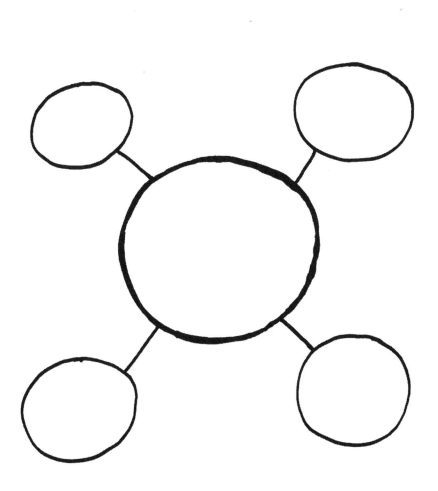

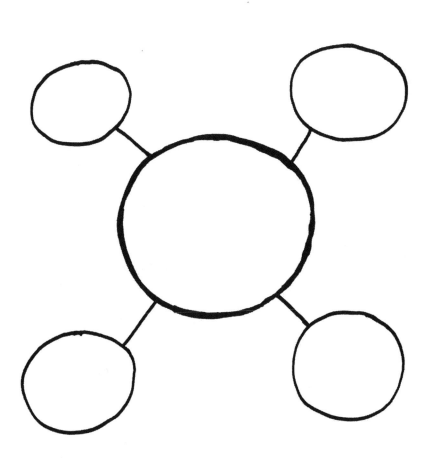

Now that you have a maximum of three categories and 12 potential sub-categories, these are the things you need to focus on. Nothing else. Get really good at doing just these things. Become exceptional, world class. You want to get so good that when someone says, "Who should I call to play guitar on my daughter's bubblegum pop record?" They immediately think of you.

Niche Please!

This idea of niching down may seem counterintuitive. "You want me to say *no* to gigs? Are you crazy?!" I know the idea of saying no to a gig is scary and right now it might seem foolish. But if you focus on honing the skills you've identified here, you will eventually become *the* person to call for that skill. This is something Peter Dyer talks about in his interview (up next!). I've always known him as the "Crazy Synth Guy," but he's also toured the world with artists like Mariah Carey and Aloe Blacc. That synth niche has scored him tons of work.

One of my niche skills is upright bass. Electric bass players are a dime a dozen (even the guitar players reading this are thinking, "Yeah, I could do that,") but someone who can play the upright bass really well is less common. I get called for a lot of classical and jazz gigs, but I also hear from acoustic singer-songwriters who want the sound of an upright bass, but the feel of an electric bass player. I've become one of the first names that some people mention when they hear someone say, "I need an upright bass player for _____."

For me, "We're going for a Mumford & Sons kind of vibe,"
are the 10 greatest words in the English language.

If you want to become the go-to person, develop your two or three niche skills and sub-skills. Become so good at them that hiring you is a no-brainer.

WARNING: Don't niche down so far that you become unhirable! Becoming "the late-13th century north-eastern Irish bagpipe player in the greater Tucson area" will ensure that you get the call, but that call will come *maaaaybe* once, if ever.

You can't do everything, so stop trying. But you will need to do more than one thing to make it as a Startup Musician. Decide what those two or three big things are and get incredible at them. Become the person to call for that thing.

And who knows, Riverdance could make a comeback, right?

CHAPTER 5
CRAZY SYNTHS & CURIOSITY w/ PETER DYER

Remember when you *first* started playing music? Remember how magical everything felt? When I learned how to play "Hot Cross Buns" on the piano at age five, you couldn't tell me *nothing*. I was a freaking boss. It felt amazing to press a key and produce a sound, and that sense of wonder propelled me deeper into music as I tried to satisfy my curiosity.

Then I discovered the bass, then GarageBand, then MIDI keyboards, my wonder growing with each new element. As musicians, I think it's a feeling we all go through, and it's an important step on the journey toward becoming a professional musician. That feeling is the thing you chase, the reason you keep at it, devote yourself to your craft, and make a career out of music.

For some people that feeling plateaus. They figure out how to do a bunch of really cool stuff, and still enjoy doing it, but other stuff gets in the way. The wonder and curiosity fade into the background.

Peter Dyer is not that guy. Peter is the physical embodiment of musical curiosity run amok. His never-ending fascination with keyboards has led him to become an expert and consequently, an in-demand performer.

Peter has toured with Mariah Carey, Aloe Blacc, St. Vincent, Adam Lambert, and Aviccii, so, you know, not a big deal. You've probably heard him play, even if you've never seen his face, maybe from one of his many live projects, records he's played on, or his iPhone commercial.

We sat down in his home studio in Long Beach (California), a room filled floor to ceiling with synthesizers. To the right is the iMac that connects them all. To the left is a box of two-dozen modular synths chained together by colorful cables. I don't understand anything about it other than the fact that there is *no way* they'd let you take that on an airplane.

♯ ♯ ♯

What kinds of things make up your job?

I am probably 70% a live performing and touring keyboardist, and then maybe 25% studio stuff and I don't know what that last 5% is...chart making for myself I guess. Yeah, it's mostly studio and playing live.

What is one thing you are particularly good at?

Synth stuff and sound design, but being able to do that in a live setting as well.

This is perhaps the most underwhelming sentence you have ever read, but it is the simplest way to describe what Peter Dyer does without being boastful.

So let me go ahead and boast for him. Peter has been called an "evil musical genius" and he has an uncanny ability to create and match synth sounds. He has an extensive knowledge of synthesizers and is a great performer. He plays very tastefully, even though he's probably only using a fraction of his musical and technical knowledge.

What do you mean by sound design for a live setting?

There's all of the sound design stuff you can do at home, and you can make a billion tracks for people, but I feel like I excel at being able to put it on the road too rather than just being a pianist, or pulling up a Rhodes patch, or something. It's matching sounds and track playback with keys and that whole bit.

What does an average week of work look like for you?

There are no averages. October it was all travel, all gigs, all the time, so maybe driving to LAX? An average workweek? It's driving around LA to rehearsals during the day. In the morning I'm probably learning the songs I was sent the night before or something. Making charts and making patches, and then if there's a gig in town, that would be the evening. Traveling is usually at least three days because it's usually fly, play, fly. That's half a week right there.

So what was your October like?

It was a week in New York with Aloe Blacc for some private shows and then I came home. Then I went to some rehearsals for Adam Lambert. I left the next week, did some TV shows in New York, and then came back. I got home, took a shower and drove out to play for Crystal Lewis in the valley. Then I went to New York again with this girl, Monogem, for a CMJ fest and then came home.

Is most of your work done away from LA?

Lately it seems to be performance, and away from LA.

Do you have any regular stuff you work on while you're out of town but not playing?

Definitely. I try a lot to stay plugged in and not just shut down when I'm out. I do a lot of tracks and production on the road. Synth stuff is a lot easier than other instruments to do mobile. Usually I'll try to get a project started here so I can take it on the road. Then I can do all the editing and maybe some synth stuff that I don't want some hardware for when I'm sitting in a green room for four hours.

I actually get a little motion sickness on busses so I can't work too well on them. But in a green room I try to set up a station. Last summer with Aloe Blacc when we were opening for Bruno Mars for a couple months we would be in these stadiums and I set up a little corner in the dressing room with a little power station. If you have your interface, your headphones, a controller, and a USB dock, you can make an album and put it out on the Internet the next day if you really want to. The technology is pretty amazing now.

So every week is a little different?

Lots of road stuff seems to be the theme this year.

In regards to your studio work, is that primarily on the road or in LA?

There are other studios, but it's mostly here in LA. Like last week, I was at a studio in Burbank (California) for the week. That was a lot of fun. Big budget studio. But usually somebody will come to my place and kind of produce it through me or they'll email me and give me some directions and references. Then it'll go back and forth on Dropbox like, "Can you change this? Can you change that?" I do a lot of that. I have the satellite station here at home.

Peter motions to the room that we're currently in, the one whose walls are lined with synths. He calls it the Forbidden Playpen.

What does your actual "work" look like?

Getting the album or the MP3s from the artist and then immediately absorbing them; listening in the car, listening at home, just trying to digest it passively first. Also trying to find some references as I'm listening; other things that are like it to get in that mood, like Al Green for Aloe was a big one, or Bill Withers, Sam Cooke, those were influences that he liked. So if I listen to those, it would inform my choices rather than just playing the album and making a chart.

My charts are kind of strange and crude because they can't just be notes, they'll be like, "and then open the envelope here and then take the pedal and switch it around and open the filter here and then if you do the split here, the strings come in at this top line here and hold it." So I'll make those charts and figure out what parts I can pull off to cover the spirit of the song. For some tracks, there's just too much. Then it kind of molds into a part and you go into rehearsal and hopefully execute it really well.

Do you have any sort of regular schedule or routines?

My morning routine is going through synth forums and music tech websites trying to keep up with stuff, see what new developments have happened, and listening to new music, especially big albums that people are gonna reference for tracks or shows. I like to keep up to speed with the industry as best I can. So that's the morning. Sometimes I practice. I don't practice enough.

Technology changes at an alarmingly fast rate and new music comes out every single day. Keeping up with all of it isn't just fun and games for Peter; he views it as an essential part of his job. Perhaps this is what has brought him to "evil musical genius" status.

Do you have any non-music hobbies?

There's a very thin line between my music stuff and the other fun stuff I have. Like the modular synth I have over there is music-ish, but I do it for the joy. It's not like, "I'm gonna get this on the track." Actually, it *has* made it on a few tracks. I don't know, watching *Star Trek*? I call this room the Forbidden Playpen because I'm a big fan of the movie *Forbidden Planet.* I'm into recorded music history, I guess, and listening to music. I don't have any other hobbies. Oh! Playing Zelda!

I have no idea how that modular synth in the corner works; it's just knobs and cables. But Peter gets it. While it's not uncommon for professional musicians to not have many non-music hobbies, I think for Peter, music is his profession and his hobby.

What is your personal life like?

Married, four years. We rent this house close to my lady's work in Long Beach and it's big enough for me to have a studio space, and another room for all the vintage big boards, and a garage. So that's nice.

Is your wife also a musician?

She is. She's a very different musician though. She's an accompanist for the Long Beach School District and she plays for a Catholic church. She does jazz arranging for vocal jazz choirs and she's a reader, a reader and a writer of more traditional styles.

So you both play piano but at very different ends of the spectrum?

I'm pretty bad at piano. I play synthesizers.

What is the hardest part about being a freelance musician?

The up and down of it. You were asking earlier about the routine and it's hard to get a routine going because these schedules are not routine. You'll be gone for a month and then you'll come home and maybe there won't be any work for two weeks. So during those two weeks I've got to mobilize for future options or try to line up future songs or gigs. It's a lot of up and down, even emotionally. If you're prepared for that, it's not so bad.

There's a concept called Imposter Syndrome where people who really excel at something feel like they're getting away with it. They have a constant uneasy feeling that they're going to be exposed as a phony and their career will be over. Peter and I talked about this weird feeling, like during those two weeks without regular music work when you feel like your career is over and you're tempted to call Terry from Best Buy. This emotional rollercoaster comes with being a freelancer of any kind, and it's something we all have to learn to live with.

I do have to remind myself of that. If you're working, you don't feel it as much, but I think it goes with the territory. You just have to remind yourself that you're in the middle of this weird career, and you're doing it right now. It's not later; you're doing it now.

If you could play one show with one artist, dead or alive, who would it be?

I would probably want to jam with Tangerine Dream back in like, 1976. They would just bring out big modulars and twist a few knobs and then let them play themselves. Or maybe Emerson, Lake & Palmer.

You only get one! This isn't a super show!

Can't they do it together? Same year? Not a super show?

Peter Dyer is not only great at what he does, he has an infinite curiosity about his instrument that inspires you to go deeper on your own instrument. He continually raises the bar on his musical abilities, partially for his own career, but mainly because it's just a whole lot of fun.

Update: Since recording this interview, Peter has gone on to join the American Idol band (in case you were wondering when we were gonna talk about that picture).

CHAPTER 6
LOOKING AS GREAT AS YOU SOUND

It Takes Money to Make Money

If you're anything like me, those words make your heart sink. Musicians don't have much money as it is! Why do we have to go spend thousands of dollars on equipment and clothes, just to get gigs that help us barely make rent? Good question.

Here's the deal. You don't *need* to spend thousands of dollars, but you do need a few things to get your startup up and running. Gig clothes are one of those things.

Remember your college days? They were fun. You could stay up as late as you wanted, type a paper 20 minutes before turning it in, and wear pajama pants to class. Well my friend, those days are over. It's time to start looking like a professional musician. Here's where to start.

Every musician, regardless of what type of music you play, will need these essential items at some point and they don't have to break the bank. Pick these up now and be prepared for any gig rather than frantically searching for a Target between sound check and the performance.

The Gentleman's Essentials

A Crisp White Dress Shirt

"Oh, but I already have one of those that my Dad gave me…"

No. That thing is faded, the collar is dirty, and you're afraid to raise your arms. You need a new one.

There are many different styles when it comes to dress shirts, but what you need is a plain white cotton point-collar dress shirt. This is invaluable. Spend a little money on a decent one. Take care of it, and you'll look great for *years*. Try not to spill anything on it, hang dry it, and you'll be golden. There is nothing better than a man dressed in a crisp white shirt.

Also, you're a grown up now; tuck it in.

Black Dress Pants

Your Dickies® are fine for hanging out, but you need a proper pair of trousers to go with your crisp white dress shirt. You're looking for a pair of no pattern, no pleats, no cuffs black dress pants. Patterns come and go and can be difficult to match with a jacket. Pleated pants make you look like your Grandpa (unless that's your thing). Cuffs can be cool, but are a bolder statement. Plus, they could go out of style soon.

For dress pants, head over to a store like Nordstrom Rack[10]. While you're there, get the legs hemmed to fit you perfectly. You'll thank me later.

A Black Suit Jacket

This will complete your outfit. If buying a complete suit is too expensive right now, buy your jacket and pants separately. Just remember to keep the patterns to a minimum so they match. You probably need a slightly smaller size jacket than you think. Most men wear jackets that are a little too big. Go ahead and get measured for a proper fit. They do that at the store (also Nordstrom Rack). Experiment with a few different cuts and styles until you find one that's right for you.

---

[10] I am not endorsed by Nordstrom Rack and receive no money in exchange for mentioning them in this chapter. In fact, even though I mention them four times, they still insist that I give them money in exchange for quality clothes and shoes.

A Crisp Black Dress Shirt

Every musician also needs a black dress shirt. The rules here are a little looser than with the white shirt, but you still want a shirt that looks sharp and isn't too loud. Go for quality on this one too. You want it to last you a long time.

Black Dress Shoes

I rocked Payless dress shoes for years. When I finally caved and bought a nice pair of $90 dress shoes, my whole world changed. They're my most comfortable pair of shoes. Considering that you're going to be standing in your dress shoes for hundreds of hours, it's important to invest in quality and comfort. I've had mine for years and they still look great. Nordstrom Rack again for the win.

Black Socks

You're not Michael Jackson, sorry. You need black socks. Get a few pairs so you don't end up pulling a stinky pair out of the laundry basket at the last minute.

A Black Tie

This is the tie you'll wear more than any other tie. Do yourself a favor and learn how to tie it well.

A Black Belt

If your pants have belt loops (and they do), then your pants need a belt. Do musicians really not know this? You'd be surprised. Get a black dress belt. Your belt loops will thank you.

Black Jeans

You won't always have to wear a suit. For some gigs you'll want to look a little more casual, but not like you're just some guy. For more casual work, clean black jeans say, "I'm with the band" without saying, "I've had these jeans since middle school."

A Dark Button Up Shirt

This one's not a dress shirt and doesn't necessarily have to be black. This shirt is going to pair with your black jeans. Shoot for somewhere between black dress shirt and the bro "going out" shirt. You want something dark and simple that looks great untucked.

Bonus Accessories

These are completely optional, but will take your look to the next level and scream professionalism.

• **Tie Clip** – This serves two purposes: it holds your tie down and makes you look damn good.

• **White Pocket Square** – This is like the cherry on top. Experiment with different folds to see what you like.

• **Wristwatch** – I know, you have a clock on your phone, but a wristwatch stands out and shows you mean business. You don't need to get a Rolex or anything super expensive. Something from Target will do just fine. Keep it relatively simple to match more of your clothes.

The Lady's Essentials

Ladies, you have a little more flexibility when it comes to a professional wardrobe based on the type of work you do. According to my wife and other female musicians, here's what you need to get going.

A Basic Black Dress

This can vary from person to person. If you're a singer, you'll definitely need a black dress. When you've got that in hand, look for a second dress that's a different color or different cut. If you play drums or have lots of gear to move, you probably want to shoot for the next option.

Black Dress Pants

Not all gigs are "black dress" gigs. And not all female musicians are "black dress" musicians. Get yourself a good pair of black dress pants. You'll look professional and have the flexibility to move around, load gear, and be comfortable.

A Black Top

I'm not even going to pretend to know the difference between a shirt, a blouse, and all the other types of women's tops, but you need a black top to pair with your black dress pants. Heed the laundering instructions on the tag to keep the shape and color on point.

Black Dress Shoes

Another flexible category that likely depends on the type of gig and your role within it. Invest in a pair of quality dress shoes that are comfortable and look good. If you need to wear heels while you perform, tuck a pair of black flats in your bag for set up and tear down. (Nordstrom Rack for the win.)

Black Jeans

Just like the guys, sometimes you want to look sharp, but not that formal. Clean black jeans will do the trick.

Casual Top

This will pair with your black jeans. It doesn't need to be black, but maybe also shouldn't be bright yellow? Use your discretion.

Caring For Your New Wardrobe

You've just sunk a chunk of change on some new

clothes and you look great! To avoid having to spend even more money in a few months on replacement clothes, do these few things to take care of your wardrobe.

When You Aren't Wearing It, Hang It Up!

You need to leave in five minutes. Where's your dress shirt? Oh yeah, at the bottom of the hamper. Not only is it as wrinkly as a bulldog, it smells like one too. To avoid this common problem, hang up your clothes when you aren't wearing them.

Wash Things Properly

Pay attention to the tags on your clothes and remember which ones are dry clean only. If you try to machine wash dry clean clothes, you'll ruin them. Take your pants to cleaners after every three or four gigs and your jacket every few months. It makes a huge difference in the way you look and it only costs a few bucks. Because you're hanging them up all the time, they'll stay looking good between dry clean visits.

Learn How to Iron

Ask your mom or jump on YouTube. Ironing takes time but is definitely worth it. Not only will it keep your clothes in good condition, you'll look like a million bucks (as opposed to only a thousand). When ironing shirts, I iron in this order: back, sleeves, collar, front. What gets seen most gets ironed last.

Polish Your Shoes

Your suit or dress looks great. It fits well and it's clean. Your shirt is freshly pressed and you can tie a wicked half Windsor knot. But those dirty, scuffed shoes will ruin the entire look. Every month or so, take a few minutes to polish up your shoes. Shoe polish is cheap and it makes a huge difference. You are someone who pays attention to the details. People notice that.

Use a Shoehorn

A shoehorn is a tool that helps slide your feet into your shoes without destroying the backs of them (your shoes, not your feet). You may think this is unnecessary, but it will make your shoes last much longer.

And speaking of shoes, if the bottoms start to wear out, have them resoled. It's cheaper than buying a new pair.

Dress for Success

I know what you're thinking, "This sounds like a lot of time and money." It is an investment, but you don't have to break the bank to dress nice. You're investing in your startup and if you buy quality clothes and take care of them, you'll save money in the long run. It's worth it to spend some money and a few extra minutes to make sure you look great at your gig. You're a professional now; it's time to dress like one.

CHAPTER 7
AUTHENTICITY & PASSION w/ VANESSA BRYNN

Photo: Marv Watson

As Vanessa Bryan walks me up a flight of stairs, she is clearly excited to show me what's behind the door at the top. "You haven't been here before, have you?" she asks. I hadn't, but I have heard lots about it. "Well, this is it!" she says, ushering me in. "Welcome to the studio!"

Vanessa is a singer who performs live and does studio sessions, voiceover work, and acting. She also opened her own academy, Music Lessons Los Angeles. That's where we've decided to meet for our interview, as it has become her new home base.

We pass instruments hanging on the walls and the control room and head into the main lobby. Vanessa explains that she and her business partner built everything themselves: the studio space, the soundproof doors, the wood paneling on the walls, they built all of it. Her voice reveals not only how excited she is to show me this space, but also how proud she is of the music school they're building and the students they're able to work with.

We sit down in her office, and just as we're about to start the interview, her business partner launches into rehearsal in the room next to us. ("Lovefool" by The Cardigans with live guitar over top). "Is that going to be a problem?" Vanessa asks. Nope. I love this song.

#

What kinds of things make up your job?

I act, I perform, and I own the school that I teach at so there's also a lot of invoicing and scheduling, answering phone calls, and paying my teachers. I do a lot of studio session work and I have many clients from over the years that just call me and at the drop of a dime I've got to be able to have a space in my calendar to go do that. It's easy to reschedule my students because they're all working as well, so I'm very lax about that. It's a lot of scheduling. A *lot* of scheduling. So much scheduling. Writing, um, rehearsing, and learning songs. It takes up a lot of time.

What is one thing you are particularly good at?

I think that my expertise really comes with performing, being on stage. There's a real art to being able to manipulate the atmosphere to connect with the audience. For me, that's something that I've always been able to do. Just kind of being able to lose myself in the moment, in the lyrics, in the music, and see myself from the audience's point of view, and create a very visual and dynamic performance. For me, that's the most important thing about being a performer, and I feel like that's what I do best."

Vanessa is one of the best singers I've ever played with. She has the ability to bring life to a song and make the audience feel connected to the band. And she doesn't do any of the things that annoy the other musicians. She stays heads up, knows her keys, knows her forms, and always gives 100%. She is everything an instrumentalist could want in a singer.

What does your average week of work look like?

Average? There is no average workweek. It's very sporadic. I try to wake up in time before my first appointment, whenever that happens to be; it can be at noon, it can be at two, it can be any time really. Wake up to be able to go to the gym, do things that I need to do as a human being just to keep my sanity. Every once in a while, like this morning, I get a call for an audition. I had to wake up early, get camera ready, be downtown, and do the audition in time to make it back for my appointments with my students. Then sometimes I have a studio session. It might be here or with other clients I have in the area so I'll have to run to that, then maybe a rehearsal at night.

I love what I do and I could consider myself a workaholic. If I have the time and space to get something done, I usually do it. It can be exhausting because my week is just jam-packed with all these little things that I try to fit into my schedule. I have to schedule days off, and that's kind of how I do that. It's crazy.

Do you have any sort of regular schedule or routines?

Any time that I've tried to work a routine into my schedule it's never worked. It just doesn't work for me. I get a call or a text and it throws a wrench into the entire thing. So I've learned to kind of live moment to moment. There's no way that I could schedule anything outside of work. You have your friend saying, "Hey, I'm having a dinner on Saturday," and I'm gonna say, "I would love to," and I really would love to. If I can be there I will be, but last minute gigs are thrown in or you're scheduled for an audition or a rehearsal or something comes up and that's basically the normal for me. Any time I try to set up a routine it just gets annihilated, so I don't even try to do that anymore.

If you need a day off how far out would you try to figure that out?

I basically look at my schedule the day before and say, "When do I have time to do this?" and then I have to make that sacrifice. Do I have to wake up early to do that? Do I have to stay up extra late to do that? For me, time is really precious and I try to schedule everything in a block of time so I can have some rest in the morning and be able to sleep at night. If something is important to me, such as being able to make my own dinner, or seeing a friend, or going to game night, I try to pack everything into this schedule that's just back to back to back to back and then I'm done. It seems to work for me.

What does your actual "work" look like?

With the students, I like to work through the different genres that they love. In getting to know their voice I can come up with song suggestions that would be great for them to work toward. They want grit in their voice, they want runs, any type of stuff like that, so I do a lot of listening to new music, music that they like, to prepare for them when they come in.

When it comes to auditions and acting, those are all last minute things. Being camera ready takes a lot of time. This morning I got a last minute call for an audition so I had to wash my hair, do my face, and dress up. For anything on camera, you have to be the best version of yourself. For a lot people, especially for women in this industry, it's very outward. To portray myself at my highest ability I also have to portray myself as if I was gig ready. That whole persona is important.

Rehearsal... I have a rehearsal tonight. I have 10 songs I have to learn. So in between everything else I'm listening, writing up the lyrics, making a word document on my iPad. It takes time and a lot of preparation.

If I have a studio session and it's in the morning, I have to wake up two hours before I even start warming up because with the voice, your body is your instrument. Morning sessions are very difficult but even if it's an afternoon session, I have to prepare. I have to have warm tea, I have to make sure that I haven't eaten a big meal right before. A lot of thought goes into being able to use your voice as an instrument. If I have a late night gig I have to schedule some way to sleep in a little bit extra the next the morning or have a block in the middle of the day when I can go home and take a nap. My voice just does not work if it's tired.

Do you have any non-music hobbies?

Uh... that's a really good question. Hobbies? Like something that I make time to do? When I have time, I love to go bowling, I love to have game nights, I love to have dinner parties, all of those things. With the type of career and life that I have, most of my friends are musicians so I like being able to see them and hang out with them. I go to their gigs and hang in the background and rest and enjoy their music. That's kind of like a non-music-related hobby, right?

I love to be outdoorsy. I don't find a whole lot of time for these things but when I do have time, I go pretty hard. I love cooking, food, and parties, anything that gets a whole bunch of friends together. When you get a whole bunch of musicians together, make sure there's not an instrument in reach, and that's basically it.

And forced vacations! Forced vacations are the best! When you have to go out of town or you're in a different state, nobody knows you and you're just with your family or whomever you're visiting, those are the best because there's no way I could be like, "I know I took the day off but this session came up so I gotta take it." Forced vacations are probably my favorite way to do something not music related.

Outside of music stuff, what does your life look like?

I have a one-bedroom apartment here in North Hollywood (California). I'm divorced from way back in the day and I am currently in a relationship, which is fantastic. He is a musician who does the same thing I do and it's really great to have someone who understands your schedule and respects the type of lifestyle that being a professional musician requires. I've got my apartment, my car, and my school here. My family is in Alaska and I visit them when I can.

Since Vanessa mentioned the benefits of dating another musician, I had to ask…

Have you dated non-musicians before and were there challenges with that?

I think the life of a musician is pretty great. You're doing what you love and it's so rewarding. No matter how dog tired you are, no matter how much work it takes to get ready, or how much performing takes out of you, you give everything that you've got on stage. It's just such a joy, it's such a passion, and you live for that.

When you date a non-musician, in the beginning they see that in you and they're attracted to that type of energy. But there's this unspoken thing where you need to kind of appear *available* on stage, especially when you have a normal gig tied to an establishment, because people are attracted to that. It's your job to bring people in, to create this energy where people think you're singing just for them. When you're an artist you're creating a connection with whoever you're working with and your partner may feel like that's inappropriate or that *they're* not getting that connection.

Then with all the gigs and the networking you need to do to keep your face and your name out there, you're essentially selling your craft all the time. With a non-musician, it wears on the relationship. And if they're someone who works a nine-to-five, and you're working at night and coming home at what, two-o-clock in the morning? It just doesn't work.

When it gets down to the heart of what it means to be a musician, which is the love, the passion, the drive for *this life*, it can be very difficult when someone says, "I don't like your life anymore because it interferes with our relationship." You become fiercely aware of this divide. And then what do you give up?

I married a non-musician and that's what happened so I gave up music. I got a job leasing apartments for federally subsidized housing. I got a cushy two-bedroom apartment for free and I was making this incredible wage, but I died every single day. I was so, so unhappy and I felt like I lost myself. After a year I just couldn't do it anymore. I quit that job and moved back to LA. I started getting back into music again, and I found myself, but within that process, my marriage started deteriorating. I know that I could never do that again.

Dating someone who *is* a musician and knows your world, is so freeing, especially if you can inspire each other and work together. That's crazy! It's really inspiring and it creates something that's deeper. It's a better connection because you're on the same page.

What is the hardest part about being a freelance musician?

This is a difficult life. It's not for the faint of heart, that's for sure. You have to truly love it. You have to just love it because there are so many difficult parts.

First of all there's the constant hustle because you have to create this work for yourself and it's exhausting. But then the work drops off and you struggle to get as much work as possible in order to float yourself through those times. You never know when you're gonna be slammed and then it all dries up for whatever reason. It's just the motion of the ocean, these waves.

Another difficult part is spending time with friends and family. You have to choose whether you're going to take work or let it go to spend time with them. Does your family really understand why you can't make it to your grandmother's birthday again? Does your best friend from high school get that the double gig the weekend of her bachelorette party is gonna carry you through the end of the month? You have to develop the awareness in your career to be able to say, "If I can be there, I will. If I can't, I can't," and it's difficult when they don't understand.

You have to be a bulldog. You have to be a warrior for what you want because younger musicians are coming up, new bands are forming, and you just never know. I feel like it always comes down to just loving it. You have to love it and fight for it because you end up having to make difficult decisions in order to maintain your career.

What about New Year's Eve? Every musician on earth works New Year's Eve. Your job is to be there, to create the atmosphere, to be the holiday. You can't spend these holidays or special events with the people that you care about, your family, or friends, or partner, but you do spend it with your musician family.

And that's one of the greatest things about being a musician; we spend so much time with each other that we become family. That's one of the most beautiful things, I think. I hear so many people talk about how they hate their job and then I get to show up to work and hug people and say, "Let's make music!" How great is that?

If you could play one show with one artist, dead or alive, who would it be?

I'm going with Tina Turner and Janis Joplin. And you know why? Because those two women have the ability to just give absolutely everything that they have: raw, real, disgusting and nasty, and loving, and wild. They give up everything on stage. They're pure performers. I absolutely love that.

They're fearless. To be able to share the stage with one of those women would be an incredible honor. It would up my game. I would learn so much. They're just fierce, you know? That's the type of energy that I try to bring to every gig. Whether it's a ballad, a rock tune, a crooning tune, what type of energy can I put into this that allows me to just be one with the song?

Performing, especially as a singer, is telling a story with a melody. You have to connect with what you're saying, otherwise, what are you doing? The singer is the human component to the band and the audience is also human. Your body is your instrument and you're speaking their language. They *feel* the music. If you connect with someone in the audience and you're truly looking at them, and you're singing your heart out to them, *everyone* will share that experience.

Vanessa knows what she needs to do to be a great singer and she does it every time she performs. She also knows what she needs to do to be a great musician. Whether she's performing, recording, or teaching, Vanessa brings a deep love and passion for music with her. It's what sets her apart from other singers and it gets her a lot of work.

NEWS FLASH: Since recording this interview, Vanessa Bryan has been touring with Idina Menzel as a background singer and guitarist. Did you know she could play the guitar? Me neither.

CHAPTER 8
www.pleasehireme.com

You Need a Website

You're not supposed to judge a book by its cover (You totally judged *this* book by its cover before you opened it, didn't you?), but we all do it. And some kind of book cover is better than no cover at all. That's your website, it's your cover. If you have a killer website that features great photos and audio clips of you performing, people are more likely to hire you because they know what you look and sound like.

Having a website also puts all of your information in one spot and conveniently directs the people searching for you to the stuff you *want* them to see. This way, when someone says, "Can I hear a recording of you?" you can direct that person to your website without having to send them individual files. *And* they won't stumble across that video of you auditioning for the Kraft Macaroni & Cheese commercial when you were 12. At least not right away.

Thanks again to my brother Ryan for uploading a personal family video to YouTube, sending the link to all of my friends, and refusing to remove it for, 10 years now?

But web design is this big, complicated, scary thing that you don't know how to do, right? Don't worry, you don't need to have a graphic design or information technology degree, or pay tons of money, to get a great website up and running.

What You Need to Get Started

Before you start messing around with themes, fonts, and domain names, you need to get all of your content together. There's no point having a website if there's nothing on it. Here's what you need to get started.

Photos

People want to see what you look like. Scour your digital world for the best photos of you. Look for photos that are great shots of you playing or that represent you well. If you don't have any good photos of yourself, don't worry. I'll bet you have a friend who just started a photography business (using their first and middle names). Talk to them about doing a photoshoot. Maybe you could trade services, or you can shell out a little money. It'll be worth it, I promise.

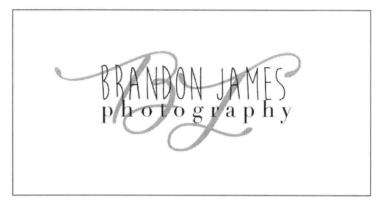

The card for my new side business. What do you think?

Audio

You *are* a musician after all. The audio files are the most important part. Gather any recordings you've done in the past few years. If you don't have anything workable, try taking a free recording session, just to get the finished recording. As a musician, you specifically deal with creating audio so these recordings need to sound great.

Video

This is optional, but a nice touch. Video combines audio with the ability to see you performing live. If you've already got some videos on YouTube, grab those links. If you've got video clips from your recitals, upload them. If you don't feel 100% about the videos you've got, don't use them. It's better to have no video at all than clips of your high school marching band practice shot on a Motorola Razr.

Bio

These always feel weird to write, don't they? You have to think in the third person and you have to make yourself sound really good. Don't be shy. The person reading your bio needs to know that you can handle the gig, whatever that may be. Be honest, confident, and persuasive. Talk about cool gigs that you've done, your education, and any other relevant details. Brief writing is definitely the trend right now with texts, Tweets, and emails so aim for about 150 words.

MVP

Remember that minimum viable product we talked about several chapters back? (You made some lists and promised me you'd work on these things until you were the best in the business.) Your website is a good place to mention them. Be clear and concise about the type of work you want to do.

Contact Information

They found you. They love you! They want to hire you! But they can't reach you. Make sure that your email address and phone number are current and easy to find.

But I Don't I Know Anything About Web Design!

That's okay! You are fortunate enough to be launching your startup in era when plenty of great drag-and-drop website services exist to help you out. No coding required!

My personal recommendation is Squarespace. For a few bucks a month, you get a website that looks great, holds all your stuff, is mobile responsive (looks good on phones), and is incredibly easy to set up. Plus, its templates are pretty slick.

But, if you're planning to do more web-based stuff as one of your MVPs down the road, then a WordPress self-hosted site is the way to go. It takes a little more work to learn how WordPress works, but once you've got the hang of it, the possibilities are endless. If you decide to go the WordPress route, visit www.startupmusician.co/website for my free tutorial.

HOWTOCHOOSEADOMAIN.BIZ

Best-case scenario, your domain would be YourName.com, but as time goes on the shorter .coms are harder to get. If you can't get the .com for your first and last name, you have a few options:

• Add a middle initial (RobMThomas.com).
• Add your instrument (RobThomasVocals.com), although this could limit you in the future if you want to expand beyond just playing.
• Add "music" to the end (RobThomasMusic.com).

Shorter domain names are preferable to longer ones. "www.brandonshawisagoodbassplayerandyoushouldhirehim.com" may be available, but no one will remember that, including you.

If you can't make it work with a .com domain, your next option is to change the extension at the end. Startup Musician's website is www.startupmusician.co simply because the .com wasn't available. I picked .co because it felt like my coolest option among the sea of .net, .org, and .biz. As the .coms fill up they've started opening up new extensions like .limo, .plumbing, and even .sucks; but why would you do that to yourself?

No matter which web company you choose, you'll probably get your domain for a free year when you sign up. If they give you the option of purchasing domain privacy, you should absolutely pay for that. Domain privacy lists the hosting company's contact information for the website's registration (behind the scenes stuff) instead of your personal contact info. This will ensure that you don't get a constant barrage of calls and emails from people offering "maximum website development ability." Trust me, it's worth the money.

But _____ Doesn't Have A Website and He's Doing Just Fine?!

True, not all musicians have websites, including some big name players. But you're not them. You're you. You need to get your name out there and give people the best representation of who you are and what you do! So go sign up for Squarespace or WordPress and get to work!

When you're finished making your website, email me the link at brandon@startupmusician.co. I'd love to check it out!

CHAPTER 9
GUITAR & OPTIONS W/ HUBIE WANG

Photo: DJ Primetime

In college it seemed like *everyone* played guitar. Even *I* had a guitar. To this day I can only play open chords, or if I'm feeling really fancy, Incubus' timeless masterpiece, "Drive". Think of how many kids there are in the world that play guitar and want to be a rock star. Little Brice sits in his room practicing "Seven Nation Army" day in and day out, usually late into the night. I know this because I live in the apartment right above Brice and he NEVER stops playing that song! The cool thing is that some of the kids who dream of making a living in music actually do. Hubie Wang is one of them.

Hubie is one of the kindest people you could meet. He's also a terrific guitar player who has worked with Nik West and Jason Mraz, had his music featured on VH1 and MTV, and knows more songs than just "Seven Nation Army" (I'm looking at you, Brice). Hubie and I sat down in his Culver City (California) apartment to chat about guitar, recording projects, and his pet tortoise, Ryan.

What kinds of things make up your job?

I'd say it's a combination of performing (whether that's local stuff or the occasional tour), studio stuff (recording guitars for other artists or maybe doing some writing and composing), and teaching. Depending on the week or the situation, the focus kind of fluctuates. This week there's a lot more playing than usual but who knows, next week I might try to do a little bit more recording for a couple of deadlines I've got.

When you do recordings, do you go into a studio or record from home?

It's about half and half. I do a lot of recording at home when it comes to working with specific producers. They send me material and say, "Hey can you replace the acoustic guitar on this for this artist I'm working with, and also add a bunch of electric stuff?" I'll do that from home. Although there's a producer that I work with pretty closely, he's sort of mentoring me as I'm trying to get more into that world, and I'll try to go to his studio as often as I can to learn by watching him. I'll lay down guitars and whatever else he may need over at his place.

What is one thing you are particularly good at?

I would probably say rhythmic guitar playing. There are so many guitar players out here (*Brice*) and a lot of them are amazing at playing leads and solos (*not Brice*). I am probably not the best at the kind of stuff. I always tell artists and anybody that I play with, "I don't ever need a solo." What I *am* good at is playing grooves, playing rhythmic stuff. Usually that means R&B, or pop, or funk music. I think I'm best at that and I try to get myself in situations where I can do as much of that as possible.

I think I'm particularly strong in that area because I grew up playing drums. I was pretty into it. In high school I was in drum line, so I think I'm more sensitive to rhythm than the average guitar player. If there's a gig where there's a lot of R&B or funk stuff, that's my favorite thing to do.

Having played with Hubie many times, I can attest to this. During a gig, he's more concerned about the overall feel of the music than trying to insert multiple guitar solos. This, plus the fact that he's so easy to get along with make him a no brainer to call when you need a guitar player.

Where do you teach?

I was teaching through an academy for a little while but I recently gave that up because I was traveling a lot and that made it really hard to have regular students; it wasn't really fair for them. In that situation I was probably doing half house calls [going to the student] and half students coming over here to the home studio.

Now I've just got a couple students. One of them I am

now trying to do on Skype; hopefully that'll work. It's for a student who's also an artist so he's on the road a lot, and he lives in Missouri. So that's going to be something new for me.

I don't do a lot of house calls anymore even though they usually pay a little bit better because it ended up being a lot of travel time and it just didn't seem as worth it. In this season, it just doesn't make as much sense for me to be on the road doing that.

What does an average week of work look like for you?

A couple of days out of the week will have afternoon rehearsals for some sort of a situation, like an original artist. If we've got a gig this week we'll maybe rehearse twice during the week. Usually my evenings through the first half of the week are kind of quiet. I may either go see someone play or try to go to a local jam session.

Thursdays though Sundays are gig nights for me and I'll be doing local club stuff or church gigs on Sunday morning with the occasional corporate gig, maybe on a Saturday, or a wedding or a country gig, those will pop up every once in a while too.

I try to do the teaching whenever I can. With the students I have right now, it works because they're super flexible and I can schedule them week-to-week and postpone and reschedule as we see fit.

Then once a week I'll try to go to the studio where my producer buddy is to spend some time there and when I'm at home I'll usually try to write or record some ideas, just anything. Let's say for example this week I have a tune that I'm supposed to record some acoustic and electric guitars for, sometimes that takes a while so I try to spread that throughout the week, maybe do an hour of it here, an hour of it there. Then I'll send it to the producer and he'll probably have some notes so I'll have to redo some things. A lot of the time is spent doing that as well.

What does your prep work during the week look like?

Let's say for a gig, I'll get the call from the artist and if it's music I've never heard before they'll send me a bunch of tracks. Then I'll sit down and chart everything out by hand. For 99% of the gigs I'll see everyone using Finale®[11]; it looks super cool and clean and I always feel a little bit inadequate, but I like using a pencil and charting stuff out myself. So I'll chart out music to help me learn it and then show up to the rehearsal ready to go.

One thing that I think is interesting for guitar players, and maybe for the style of music that I play, and where music seems to be right now, is that there's a lot of electronic elements where sometimes the guitar is not even in the original song, so it's up to the guitar player to generate the parts or create space. It's kind of a weird situation where you rely a little bit more on improvisation than you think you would for your average original gig or cover gig even. Sometimes for me that means charting out a specific synth line, or a horn line, and trying to be ready for whatever that song may need. Sometimes I don't know what's important to the artist, like this particular line could be important and I didn't realize that and I didn't learn that.

A teacher once told me to "try and provide as many options as you can" so that it's up to [the artist] to determine what they want. It makes you look more prepared and more professional. But that's a challenge for guitar players, especially these tracks that have multiple guitar parts, but most of the time I'm the only guitar player on the gig. So I learn both parts and figure out how to navigate both to sort come up with my own arrangements of things. That can be

---

[11] Finale® is a sheet music making product of MakeMusic, Inc.

kind of tricky and something that may be unique to guitar players and keyboard players, more so than drummers or bass players.

Learning songs by ear and charting them out myself is something I used to hate. Why can't everything have sheet music already made?! When I realized that I would be learning new songs for the rest of my life, I decided to embrace it and get better at it. For live musicians, learning songs and being able to adapt them for a live setting is an essential part of the job.

Do you have any sort of regular schedule or routine?

I try to stay as active as possible, so in the mornings if I don't have a rehearsal that's scheduled too early I like to try to work out for 30 minutes. Sometimes that's at home. I'm a big fan of the Insanity® workouts and that Shaun T. guy, he's my hero.

I try to run errands during the day, like groceries; otherwise I don't really have too many other routine things. There was a time when I was trying to practice more. Like practice Charlie Parker heads and stuff like that. That kind of comes in waves. I'll get real excited about integrating an hour of jazz every day; that usually happens when things are kind of slow, and then something comes up and I sort of forget about it. Ideally I try to practice a little bit every day, but sometimes that doesn't always happen.

As far as days off, I think there always ends up being one day a week where I have a little more time off. I'm married and my wife has a "regular" job so I try my best to be around on weekends to enjoy time with her, but she's also super understanding when that doesn't always work out. Saturday during the day tends to be good, but the occasional wedding gig means you need to be there at 1:30 in the afternoon and the rest of your day is sort of shot. It depends.

Do you have any non-music hobbies?

I'm a casual sports fan all around. I'm wearing this (*Hubie points to his Dodgers shirt*) because I have a rehearsal after our interview and one of the guys in the band is a Padres fan, he's from San Diego (California), so the bass player asked us all to wear Dodgers gear so that we can remind him who runs this town.

What is your non-musical life like?

So I'm married to a lawyer and we don't have any kids. But we do have a pet tortoise that's living on the balcony. We got him when he was a baby and could fit in the palms of our hands and now he's about 30 pounds. He's a Calcutta tortoise, so if all goes well, he'll grow to be about 100 pounds and 100 years old. We joke that the goal is to eventually get a house with a yard so that we can raise our tortoise and he can roam freely.

On my way out, Hubie introduces me to Ryan. The outside deck is his domain, complete with a doghouse, which he probably won't fit in much longer. Despite my best efforts, Ryan did no tricks and largely ignored me. I don't blame him.

What is the hardest part about being a freelance musician?

There are a lot of hard parts, and the hardest for me is not knowing where my income may come from, not knowing what my schedule is gonna look like from month to month. I grew up being taught that stability is really important; if you go to school, and get good grades, and go to college, and get a degree, and get this job, then you're gonna be set. I kind of always had that mentality too, and when I decided to play music professionally, I think I realized pretty quickly that it's really hard to have that kind of philosophy doing this job.

So *that* I think is the trickiest part; when you have bills and expenses and you don't know how it's gonna happen, you don't know how you're gonna take care of them all. But somehow it's worked out so far and I think every day you learn a little bit more about how to handle all that. Hopefully as the years go by you get a little closer to having that stability but it's definitely a huge challenge for me. I worry about it all the time, but at the same time I can't really picture myself doing something else that would be more "safe".

If you could play one show with one artist or band, dead or alive, who would it be?

I've been asked this before and my default answer used to be Prince or Michael Jackson or something like that, but lately I've been thinking that the most fulfilling situation for me would be to play with the Red Hot Chili Peppers in the early to mid-90s. Hearing some of that Red Hot Chili Pepper stuff was a big, musically life-changing moment for me because that was the first time I heard the guitar being played in a different way where it was more rhythmic. It wasn't just like louder, faster, bigger, it was more…I don't know; there was more finesse to it.

I had a teacher who once said, "We all grew up in the same garage band," and I think it's totally accurate. We all grew up playing the same songs. Now that I'm a teacher, I have students who want to learn stuff, and it's the same songs that I wanted to learn when I was 12 years old. It's ACDC and Guns N' Roses, all this like classic stuff. I think 99% of all guitarists start there but we all end up in different places.

Any final thoughts?

I have to say it's a struggle a lot of the time but it's worth it. It's definitely not as sexy as I thought it would be when I was 12 years old (*hear that, Brice?*) but it's awesome and hopefully this interview will help give someone some insight on how to jump in and to be a part of this whole thing.

I'm going to see if Brice wants to take lessons with Hubie and learn LITERALLY ANY OTHER SONG.

CHAPTER 10
MAKING MONEY

Getting Down to Business[12]

I used to look down on business majors from my high and mighty music perch with a smug attitude, as if to say, "I'm in it for the *love* man! I'll never be like you, you corporate suit!" Although this is still something I regularly tell my old roommate, in retrospect, I could have learned a lot from them. After all, what *is* a business?

It's not an office building, a name, or even a title. At its core, a business is the act of making or providing *something* that people want and giving it to them in exchange for money. Which is exactly what you're doing as a Startup Musician.

So let's look at some practical ways that your business can make some money.

---

[12] No huns necessary.

Getting Paid

As we discussed in Finding Your Niche, your startup will probably have a few different components under the music umbrella and you can charge varying amounts of money for your services. Here are just a few ways that your startup can turn a profit. (See what I did there with my suave business speak?)

Playing Live (in town)

This is a very common service to offer, and it's dead simple. I learn songs or you give me sheet music, I show up and play them once, you pay me. This could be recurring work, or on a one-time basis.

Playing Live (touring)

This is another common service; the only difference here is that you're repeating the same work in different places. In this scenario, they are also buying your time *off* stage because you're traveling with the group.

Recording Session (in studio)

I show up to a recording studio, I play, you record me playing, and you pay me.

Remote Recording Session (at home)

You send me a track of something you've already recorded, I play it into my own home recording setup, I send it to you via Dropbox, and you send me money via PayPal/Venmo/Square Cash.

Teaching Private Lessons

There are a couple iterations of this. Either I drive to

your house or you drive to mine, I teach you how to play an instrument week by week, and you pay me. Or, a company (academy) pays me to teach you in their building, you pay them, and they pay me.

Teaching at an academy is actually a great way to jump into teaching, especially right after graduation, because it provides a pretty consistent stream of students in a set location. But after a while, you can make more money by scheduling the students yourself. There's more administrative stuff to do, but there's also more money in your pocket.

Arranging

You have a song but you need something changed (instrumentation, different chords, shortened, etc.). I change it for you, send you sheet music for it, and you pay me.

Original Composition

Your first thought may be a Mozart-type situation, but that's not what I'm talking about. Yes, some people actually do that, but a very common version of this is composing music for something else, like a commercial, movie, TV show, podcast, corporate video, or something similar.

Mixing and/or Mastering

I take a recording (see Remote Recording Session above), balance the levels, tweak minor (or major) things, sprinkle in some magic, and make it sound *goooood*.

Music Directing

This is often an extension of playing live. The music director (MD) is the person in charge of the band and helps bring the vision of the artist or show director to life.

Copy Work

Think Sibelius®[13] or Finale®. You're making sheet music for an existing song, not an original composition.

#

Listed above are just a few things that you could offer in your startup. But there's plenty more that I haven't thought of yet.

What to Charge

After you decide what your startup does, the next question to ask is, "What should I charge?"

First, the bad news: I'm not going to give you specific numbers. There is a wide range when it comes to the fees for these services and it all depends on a number of different factors. Rather than cite some numbers that vary by situation, may not apply to your situation, and will be dated as soon as you read this, I'll tell you how to figure out what to charge. I call it the two-thirds rule.

The 2/3 Rule

As musicians, we live in the space between work and play. This isn't to say that being a musician isn't *work*. We put in lots of hours practicing, learning songs, and making sure we are fully prepared for whatever work is on our plate. We do, however, get to do something much more enjoyable than sitting in a cubicle. That's *our* perk.

The perk for cubicle guy is that he knows exactly how much he's going to be paid for every day that he clocks in. That conversation happened one time on the day he accepted

---

[13] Sibelius® is a sheet music making product of Sibelius Software.

the job and he hasn't had to think about it since. You and I, on the other hand, get to repeat that conversation on a regular basis. To help think it through, I use something called the 2/3 Rule. I picked it up from a professor of mine and have lived by it ever since.

There are three factors that you should consider when deciding whether or not to take a gig. This works for almost every project (composing, teaching, etc.) but we'll use gigging as the example.

Factor No. 1: Money – How much the gig pays.

Some pay a lot, some pay very little; important to know, but not the only thing to consider.

Factor No. 2: People – The musicians you'll be playing with.

This can make a big difference on your experience. If you're going into a gig knowing that that one sax player who's a tool is going to be there, you're in for a rough night. Future you is going to *hate* past you.

Factor No. 3: Music – The type of music you'll be playing.

Is it stuff you love playing and already know? Or do you have to learn 200 songs for a jazz gig in the middle of the desert? Is it playing in a Savage Garden cover band? Again, think about future you.

Future you hates past you!

Now that you understand the three factors, here's the rule:

Every gig you take must fulfill at least two of the three factors.

In order for you to take a gig, it needs to have one of the following combinations:

- Good money + good people
- Good money + good music
- Good people + good music

It doesn't matter if you're playing "Truly Madly Deeply" for the umpteenth time if you're with your buddies and you're making good money. You'll all laugh about it later as you deposit your sweet paycheck.

It doesn't matter if that sax-playing tool is going to turn around and clap out the downbeats to you *again* if the price is right and you're playing fun music. You'll still be generally happy with the music and very happy with the check.

And it doesn't matter if you aren't getting paid very much at all if you're playing music you love with musicians you love. You're going to have a blast playing music, and that's worth enough to take it.

Occasionally, the stars will align and you'll get a gig that has all three. Enjoy that, because that's the dream.

Should I Ever Work for Free?

Now that I've outlined the two-thirds rule, I'm going to break it because sometimes it is a good idea to take free work. Think of this as the No-Thirds Rule.

If you're just starting out, and no one knows who you are, what you do, or what kind of person you are. If you're trying to be a performer, you need to get out there and get heard. If you're trying to be a mixing engineer, you need to have some of your mixes heard. If you're an arranger...you get the point.

This is the musical equivalent of the free samples they hand out at Costco. I probably wouldn't have bought a 40-pack of chicken bakes on my own, but now that I've tried a sample, dammit I've got to have more. No one is going to buy chicken bakes unless they know what they taste like, and so sometimes, you need to work for free.

In the early days of launching your startup, you won't be making much money. Don't let this discourage you; it's totally normal. Building a business takes time, whether you're selling chicken bakes or your mad keyboard skills. Focus on honing your craft, building a portfolio, and getting your work out there as much as possible.

When deciding whether or not to take a free gig, ask yourself these questions:

1. Does it pass the other two parts of the 2/3 test? (good people + good music)

2. If not, is there some other benefit I can get out of it? (Think promotional benefits, getting your name out there, free Costco samples...)

If the answer to both of these questions is "No," don't be afraid to turn it down.

I once got called for a gig that was:
- Free
- With random people
- Not fun music
- An hour away
- Lacking any other promotional opportunities
- Not serving Costco samples

There was absolutely no reason for me to take this gig, so I politely turned it down and I didn't feel bad about it. When they asked if I could refer someone who was "as good as me but who would also do it for free," then I got annoyed. But I bit my tongue, finished the conversation, and moved on.

So yeah, sometimes you play for free, and sometimes you don't. Above all remember this: you are a business. While giving free samples at Costco is a great to way gain customers, you can't give away whole boxes of chicken bakes to everyone who asks.

Will I Have to Play Music I Don't Like?

Here's an actual sentence that came out of my mouth, circa 2005: "I don't like country music. I only like *good* music, like Coldplay." Oh young Brandon, you had so much to learn.

When you first get into music and you discover just how much is out there, you pick and choose the different things that float your boat. In high school, I listened almost exclusively to bands like Coldplay and Death Cab for Cutie. To me, that was "good music," and in my limited scope, I wrote off entire genres of music. Early college was my hip-hop phase (Since I bought *Late Registration* on vinyl, this could also be called my G.O.O.D. Music phase), and shortly thereafter was my electronic phase. I even recreated the Daft Punk "Around The World" music video for my junior recital.

Junior Recital, Azusa Pacific University

I've had many genres come and go in my life but I can say with 100% certainty that I've never had a country phase. It just doesn't do it for me. But in recent years I've moved away from genre bashing. Why? Because on more than one occasion people have paid me good money to play country music. Country music paid my rent that month.

Genre hopping does have its limits (still not getting called for the authentic Latin gigs), but regardless of your personal taste, you're probably going to end up playing multiple genres including stuff that you wouldn't listen to on your own. And that's okay.

You don't have to love all of the music you're playing, but appreciate it for what it is, and play it to the best of your ability. In a great interview with the Red Bull Music Academy, Questlove talked about this regarding his DJ style and his personal taste in music.

> "I've learned, maybe last year, to just do away with the idea of "this is good music, and this is bad music." Because, you know, personally for me, I know what I personally like, my personal tastes. My personal tastes don't match my professional tastes. You know, last year I had absolutely no shame whatsoever in playing "Gangnam Style."

> You can laugh now, but nothing beats the feeling of watching a thousand execs at the Viacom Christmas party dance on tables. So it's like, well, is that a bad song, or is that an effective song? And so that's the conflict I've been having: my personal taste versus my professional taste. Because a lot of the music that I won't listen to on my personal time, I need that to work for me. It's something that I've been wrestling with. So I don't know, I

don't believe in good or bad music anymore. I just believe in what's effective and what's not effective."[14]

It's incredibly encouraging to hear someone as prolific and creative as Questlove talk about knowing his audience and what they want. If he was DJ-ing the Viacom Christmas party and played exclusively deep cut J Dilla beats, everyone would awkwardly head for the door. That's the wrong audience; they won't appreciate it. Instead he puts his personal preferences on hold, plays what they want to hear, and makes them lose their minds.

Don't write off entire genres of music because they aren't your cup of tea. Give the people what they want and play it to the best of your ability. "Gangnam Style" just might pay your bills this month.

Making Money Making Music

Making a living as a freelance musician doesn't mean you get to play exclusively the stuff that you want to play, but it does mean you get to make money while playing music. No matter what you're doing, with whom, or for how much, you're still making music for a living, and that's amazing.

If you want to become a professional musician but only make the music that you love to make, it's a little like playing the lottery. You *could* make it big and spend the rest of your life making exclusively the music that you want to make, getting paid big bucks, and vacationing at Sting's Tuscan villa. But that's a one-in-a-million kind of scenario. More likely, you'll burn out after a few years of frustration, take that traditional nine-to-five job, and continue to play music but as a hobby.

---

[14] 2013 Red Bull Music Academy (http://www.redbullmusicacademy.com/lectures/questlove-new-york-2013)

If you want to become a professional musician because you want to make a lot of money, you're also playing the lottery. While DJ Khaled may be on that magical money road, *you* will probably never be able to afford a personal chef or a beachfront house in Miami.

Success as a professional musician is somewhere in between. It's getting paid to play music you love to play *and* getting paid to play music you hate, it's playing with your friends and sometimes with saxophone guy, it's earning exactly what you're worth but also taking a free gig now and then.

It may sound intense, but would you rather work at Best Buy? If you're 10 chapters into this book, I sure hope not.

CHAPTER 11
TEACHING & FLEXIBILITY W/ JEN OIKAWA

Photo: Shannon Leith

Jen Oikawa is a pianist and keyboard player who built her startup around a few different components. She does the freelance playing you might expect from a piano player like accompanying choirs and soloists, playing for musicals, and playing with artists or for church services. She also writes music for her jazz trio and has released two albums of original music. But her start up staple is teaching piano lessons, one on one in people's homes.

For many musicians, teaching is the "Plan B". It's not what they *really* want to be doing, but it's a way to make some money, so sure, they'll teach some five year olds for a while. But Jen has the teaching thing *down*. Her teaching is incredibly organized and put together and because of that, she has a full schedule of students. I sat down with Jen to discuss her work and dive into her busy schedule.

# # #

What is your area of expertise?

As a piano teacher I think I bring something unique because I also do other things besides teaching, and the fact that I have a classical training background but I also play jazz, rock, pop, gospel, and all that kind of stuff. I bring both of those different areas of teaching to a lesson, where I think a lot of teachers are either one or the other. So my students get something that's unique and different that they can't necessarily find everywhere else.

As a performer, as a jazz musician, in my own writing and in my own group, I feel that I am able to connect with people. I don't know if it's because I have a lot of friends who aren't musicians and I feel like I'm able to connect with people who wouldn't necessarily listen to jazz but do because they know me, or because I'm able to play or perform in a way that sort of makes that more accessible. I think that's a strength.

What does an average week of work look like for you?

I would say the most consistent part of my schedule is my lessons. That can change, but right now I teach on Monday through Thursday mostly in the late afternoon and early evening. I have a few students that I teach on Wednesday morning. So my own time, as far as prepping for lessons, or bookkeeping, or scheduling, or responding to emails, that kind of stuff, I usually do in the early afternoon, then teach in the late afternoon and into the evening.

And then around that schedule I'll get to other things. Last week I was playing for a musical so I was there every night, but that's not a normal week. Or I might have a gig that I'm playing on the weekend and I need to work on music or we have a rehearsal. Or I'm scheduling my own show, different things like that. It kind of depends on each week. The teaching is pretty consistent and then I get different stuff coming around that.

How many students do you currently teach?

Right now it's 15, I think. That number has gone up and down throughout the years. The most I've had was 26 and that felt like too much. I just get burnt out with too many lessons and how much I'm giving with that. It's also harder to have the flexibility to take those other jobs if your schedule is so full with those consistent things. I think my ideal would be no more than 20. With 15 I'm still okay, I can make it [financially] and then I end up saying, "yes" to other jobs that come up so it balances itself out.

Are you giving lessons in your home or do you drive to your students?

Mostly I drive to the students although I have five students who come here. I'm single and I've always had a roommate so I've never wanted to impose that on somebody's life; to come home from work everyday to piano lessons, like, little kids playing terribly.

So I go to people's homes even though I've been in my place for a while. There was a time when I moved a lot so it felt more consistent to go to their homes. That way if I moved I didn't lose a bunch of students because now I'm in a different area. And that's an extra service that I think a lot of people really appreciate so that's kind of how that's worked out.

Finding new students is always a challenge. How have you advertised to get new students?

Actually, I've advertised very little, even in the beginning. As a piano player if you're at a church or doing something where people see you consistently playing, then people start to approach you like, "Do you teach? Can I take lessons?"

At this point getting students is all through word of mouth and references. I haven't advertised for teaching in a long time. But you might have students who graduate from high school and move on to something else or different things come up, so it kind of goes up and down.

There was a time when I was teaching out of a couple of different studios because I had been working at a church full time and then I quit that job and was trying to build up a base of students. So I was teaching at different studios to start with.

I had put something in my church newsletter, but I got like one student out of that. I started teaching when I was in high school so back then I think I put something in a community newsletter and I remember getting a couple of inquiries but no actual students from that. So I guess honestly it's always been word of mouth. When I first started out my piano teacher passed on a few students that she didn't have room to take. And then there were kids in the neighborhood. If you're doing a good job and your clients like you, that they start to tell their friends. Or if they're taking lessons people will ask them about their teacher.

People with kids who take piano lessons usually know other people with kids who want piano lessons, so word of mouth is a very effective way to get new students, especially for instruments like piano and guitar. Like many musicians, I started on piano when I was five years old (before I wised up and moved to the bass). Thinking back, we found every one of my teachers through another friend of mine who was already taking lessons with them.

If you play something a bit more unusual, like, for example, the upright bass, I've found it's a pretty similar experience. If you can make a name for yourself as the [insert instrument here] teacher in your area, the students who want to take lessons naturally gravitate toward you. You may not have as many students as someone who teaches a more common instrument, but you can still thrive as a teacher with a more niche instrument. I've had as many as 10 private upright bass students at once.

Contacting other teachers is actually a really good way to get new students because teachers who are well established usually don't have space to take new students. If they know about you then they have someone to refer those students to and I feel like that helped me a lot when I first started. There were a couple of teachers that I knew who moved out of state at the same time and both of them passed on a handful of students to me. That's actually how I got that base of students and then it grew from there. Getting connected to other teachers is probably one of the biggest ways that I was able to gather students in the beginning.

It turns out that networking is just as important for teachers as it is for performers. My former college bass teacher got a call from an upright bass student looking for a teacher. This student lived far from my teacher's house, but close to me, so he referred him to me. Five years later I'm still teaching that student and have received several more referrals through him. When I'm too busy to take on all of these students myself, I pass them on to other bass players I know. Cue "Circle of Life" from The Lion King.

What does your actual "work" look like?

I have a lot of very consistent clients so once I set the schedule in September it doesn't change much through the school year, which is nice. But setting up that schedule is sometimes challenging especially since I drive to the student's homes. I can't just be like, "Oh just slot this guy here and this guy here and this one here." It's like, "Well, this one's in Pasadena and that one's in Burbank,"[a 20-30 minute drive] so that's not going to work. I have to consider traveling distances, and their schedules, and put all of that together in a way that makes sense for them and for me.

I actually don't guarantee that I can reschedule a lesson if a student cancels. I used to guarantee that I would reschedule it at some point, but it started to get pretty tricky. When students start changing lesson times what can really mess up the schedule.

As far as prepping for lessons, with my very beginner students I know what books I'm going to start with, where we're going to begin. As they progress, then I need to think about what direction I want to take them, what kind of music might work best for them. Some of my students will request to learn certain songs and if that song makes sense on the piano then I try to seek out a good arrangement for them. There's also been a few times where I've arranged a song for a student if they really wanted to learn it. Books change and there are new ones coming out all the time, so I'm keeping track of that or checking out new stuff so I can recommend it to my students.

I also have students who do certificate evaluation so I need to make sure I know what the requirements are and that we're on track and on schedule. And then I organize two or three recitals each year. So there's booking those, setting up the program, and communicating with the students and parents.

And then there's bookkeeping and keeping track of my expenses and when I'm getting paid, and all that stuff for taxes, that's my favorite!

Do you have any sort of regular schedule or routine?

I usually try to take mornings to myself. I read, coffee, journal, obsess about life for a little bit. Even when I have extra gigs on my plate the mornings are typically the least scheduled. If I *am* playing for something, that's often on the weekend, so Fridays will often be a day off but not necessarily all the time. Sometimes I'm going to be busier; sometimes I'm not. I do go to yoga three times a week. That's fairly consistent.

Do you have any non-music hobbies?

Baking!

What is your go-to thing to bake?

Pies. If I want something fast I make these little freeform apple tarts, and if I want something complicated that's gonna take a long time then I make a chocolate cream pie.

What is your personal life like and how does that play into your musical career?

I live in an apartment and I rent. It's LA so that's rather common. I've actually been in this place for six years but before that I would move almost every year, at least every two years. So I've had a lot of roommates through that time which helps because I have consistent work, but I'm not always making a lot of money.

Having roommates is something that's been helpful for me financially and also with being single it helps having someone else in my home so I'm not spending too much time all by myself.

What is the hardest part about being a freelance musician?

Being single and being self-employed, I can end up spending a lot of time on my own. Or I'm doing one-on-one lessons with kids, which is not really social time. I think a challenge for me is finding ways to be with other people so that I don't get too isolated just sitting with my piano at home.

The other challenge is that there's not this straightforward path. There's no, "Okay. Now I'm a self-employed piano keyboard player, and this is what my life is gonna look like and this is the next step toward that very specific goal."

There's always this sort of flux, and making decisions as far as how to put all of this together. It's kind of creating what your mix and your job looks like all the time. On one hand that can be exciting and creative and on the other it can be daunting, like there's all these options I could do, but how exactly do I do them? What fits me more? What do I say yes to and what do I say no to? I feel like I could obsess about job offers for a long time. "Is that worth it? Do I want to put that work in?"

I feel the same way. There are always an infinite number of things that you could be doing. Ideas are cheap. I can think up ideas all day.

The hard part is actually making the decision to do something.

I love making plans; they make me feel secure. Knowing every possible outcome of every possible scenario gives me comfort before I dive into something. This can prevent me from making mistakes, but it can also prevent me from pursing great opportunities. While I'm on the side making plans, the pool is filled with people swimming, splashing, and shooting each other with water cannons. While I'm thinking it, they're doing it.

If you could play one show with one artist, dead or alive, who would it be?

On the one hand I can think of piano players but why would I play with piano players, unless it was like a duel. The ones I like I would definitely lose to. I think playing in a group with Oscar Peterson would have been awesome. His energy and groove and swing and all of that; to be able to experience that would have been something amazing.

Jen has managed to find the sweet spot where a freelance musician works a pretty consistent schedule. She's even found a balance between over-scheduling and flexibility to pursue her original work.

NEWS FLASH: Since we recorded this interview, Jen hit the road with Motown: the Musical on a North American tour.

CHAPTER 12
WHEN TO QUIT YOUR DAY JOB

Taking the Plunge

Jumping into being a full-time musician is a scary thing. If you're still in school, a recent graduate, or just ready to take the plunge into making music your only source of income, how do you make that transition? How do you know when you're ready to go full-time in music?

First, a couple of caveats. Somebody get me a soapbox.

There's a prevailing attitude in the professional music community that goes something like this: if you're not doing music *only*, then you're not *really* doing music. You're not a "real" musician, and you're somehow not as good as everyone else who is.

Let's get rid of that idea right now. Let's pinch our metaphorical fingers together and zoom out for a second to get some perspective.

As a Startup Musician, you are starting your own business. Literally. YOU are a business. And many businesses take *years* to become profitable. For the first several years of a business's existence, it may not make enough money to pay the bills. It may not make enough money to pay rent and it certainly won't make enough money to keep buying gear you don't really need.

# # #

A Rabbit Trail About Gear (While Still On My Soapbox)

Here's the deal. You don't need to spend thousands of dollars, but you do need gear that's good enough.

One of my favorite things is when a musician feels like they have to have all of the bells and whistles available. They buy the pick holder for the mic stand. They have the weird X-shaped guitar strap. They have *everything* that Planet Waves makes.

But this ergonomically designed strap will give me a chiropractic adjustment while I play!

That stuff is fine, but in reality you probably don't need all of it. What you *do* need is gear good enough to get the job done. I'm not saying you should be gigging around with your buddy's old Adam Levine guitar from Target. Get good gear that works, that doesn't get in the way of doing your thing, and that you actually need.

Here's my general rule of thumb: don't buy it until you really need it. I can't tell you how many purchases I've made thinking, "I'm totally going to get into this now!" only to have it sit on the bottom shelf, unused for months.

There's a middle ground between these two extremes. You probably don't need to go buy a boutique limited edition amp, but you do need to have a working amp. You don't need a Fender Custom Shop American Deluxe 8 String Guitar with Stevie Ray Vaughn's sweat mixed into the finish, but you do need to have a decent-sounding guitar. A Squire probably won't cut it.

Having halfway decent gear not only makes you sound better, it makes you look like you know what you're doing. It says to the other musicians on stage, "I'm serious about my career; this isn't just a hobby." If you're serious about being a professional musician, go get some decent gear; something that will get the job done without completely breaking the bank.

Gear is cool, but you know what's cooler? Music. Focus on being a great musician, and be happy with your rig until you have the extra money to spend on new stuff. Having a MONO case won't get you more gigs. Sounding great when you pull your instrument out of the case will.

I now return you to your previously scheduled soapbox discussion.

# # #

This is where the analogy of a musician as a startup doesn't quite line up. When you start a business or company, you usually don't make a profit for the first few years. So how do people do it? How do they make money for rent, to pay the employees, and for the cost of doing business? That money has to come from somewhere.

For many startups, the answer is investors. These are people who trade cold hard cash for a percentage of the company, hoping to strike it rich when the company takes off. For musicians there's no real equivalent to these investors (other than maybe your parents). But let's be real, if you're the dude who is "just really trying to focus on his music" all day, playing one gig a month, and *mysteriously* still able to make rent, you aren't fooling anyone. Mom and Dad are bankrolling that adventure, and it has an end date, whether you can see it or not.

For Startup Musicians, we've got to find the extra money while we build our business. This comes in the most simple, straightforward, unsexy way: getting a part-time job.

Having a part-time job takes the pressure off of having your music pay all of the bills and gives you the flexibility to continue honing your craft. It can also have *this* great side effect: it'll drive you *just* crazy enough to motivate you to build your startup ASAP so you can quit and pursue music full time.

Money in the short term, support for building your career, and motivation to grow your startup? Sounds like having a part time job is a win-win-win.

For me, it was the Apple Store. I worked there right out of college. Actually I was "working" for them even before they hired me. That is to say, I had memorized every spec of every product they had on display. I watched the Apple Keynotes religiously; they are my Super Bowl. Working there made perfect sense. I was good at it, it paid decent, and they were incredibly flexible with my schedule because they knew I was a musician.

For you, maybe it's a standard part-time job working retail or waiting tables. Maybe you'll drive for Uber or Lyft™ a few hours a week to help fill the gaps. Wherever your initial startup funding comes from, do not feel guilty about it. Kill it at your part-time job, clock out, and then get to work on your startup.

When Is It Time To Quit Your Day Job?

How do you know when you're ready to make the jump, quit your job, and go full time with music? With some analysis and a little math, we can figure this out together. There are a few questions you'll need to ask yourself first.

How Much Money Do I Need?

This might seem like a dumb question, but you actually need to figure out how much money you need every month. If you just quit your day job and "hope it all works out," you'll end up on your parents' sofa doing "video game music score research."

Rent is due on the 1st, your phone bill on the 6th, your car insurance on the 21st, and you're constantly filling your car with gas throughout the month. If you're only paying for things as they come up, you may not know how much money you actually need to survive.

Total up *all* of your monthly expenses. By "monthly expenses" I mean the *bare minimum* list of things that you actually have to pay for. Cut out your excessive visits to Chipotle and your Netflix subscription. (I've been using my brother's login for years.) Just include the absolute basic things you need to pay your bills, put gas in your second-hand Volvo, and eat cheap food at home.

To make this easy, I've included a chart for you to fill in. Write down all of your monthly expenses in the column on the left and them add them up to get your "Total Monthly Minimum".

How Much Money Do I Make Right Now?

Since freelance musicians are paid sporadically throughout the month and not every two weeks like most people with traditional jobs, you might not know how much money you actually make. The amount may surprise you.

It doesn't matter if you are gigging, teaching, recording, composing, or all of the above, total up everything you've made in the past three to four months from your various music jobs. Jot this down in the second column. Calculate the average of these months (total amount of dollars divided by number of months) and write that on the line on the right.

EXPENSES

RENT $ ___
UTILITIES $ ___
PHONE $ ___
CAR PAYMENT $ ___
CAR INSURANCE $ ___
GAS (EST.) $ ___
FOOD (EST) $ ___
HEALTH INS. $ ___
STUDENT LOANS $ ___
CREDIT CARD $ ___
OTHER $ ___

TOTAL $ ___

INCOME

LAST MONTH $ ___
2 MONTHS AGO $ ___
3 MONTHS AGO $ ___
4 MONTHS AGO $ ___
SUB-TOTAL $ ___

DIVIDE BY 4

TOTAL $ ___

Do the Math

The math here is simple. If the number in the right column is larger than your TMM in the left, things are looking good! If the left number is larger, keep plugging away at your part-time job and work on your startup whenever you can.

The Mentality

It's going to be difficult for a while, but that's not a bad thing.

You're probably going to have to eat a lot of Top Ramen®. (But at 10 cents each, how can you not?) You'll have to buy less stuff on Amazon. Worst of all, you'll have to start saying "No" to things that cost money. Let me present you with a difficult scenario.

Your friends are all going to Disneyland! Hey, that sounds fun! Oh, but that's right, your Verizon bill is due next week. But it's *Disneyland!* Yeah, you can probably make it work!

WRONG.

You cannot make it work. Disneyland will be fun, but you know what won't be, overdrawing your account because you set up autopay and forgot about it. (I have wasted *hundreds*[15] doing this.)

In this scenario, you have to make the difficult choice of not going. But, don't make a scene about it. Please don't say, "I can't afford fancy stuff like that, I'm just a broke musician." Just say, "Sorry guys, I won't be able to make it."

---

[15] Not an exaggeration.

Give Yourself A Runway

Building a music career takes time. So take as much music work as you can whenever it comes your way, while finishing school or working at Best Buy. You want to get to the point where you can barely make your work schedule because you're so busy being a musician. When you reach this critical point, as long as your numbers add up, you're ready to jump. That way, when you *do* finally quit your job, graduate, or (heaven forbid!) drop out of school, your music career will already have a running start.

Your Income Will Change Like the Wind

As a freelancer, your income won't come from a single source or on a consistent schedule. Some months you'll just barely scrape by; others you'll think to yourself, "If every month was like this I'd be rich!" And more than once you'll consider calling up Terry at Best Buy to ask for your old job back. This financial rollercoaster comes with the territory. Rollercoaster isn't even the right word because rollercoasters are fun. This is more like a financial car driven by an over-caffeinated twelve year old.

Also you should know this: As a general rule, there are some dry months as a musician:

• Live gigs are much scarcer in January and February. It just works out that way.

• Private lessons drop off during the summer months when students go on vacation or leave for summer camps.

• December is hands down the best month to be a professional musician. Everyone wants to be entertained, companies blow their year-end budget surpluses, and students give you candy!

You Need To Be Completely Broke For Awhile

If reading all of this is making you doubt that you have what it takes to be a full-time musician, don't worry; it does get better. For now though, you need to be broke.

I know that seems dumb, but let me explain.

If you're not great with money, the solution to your problem isn't just having more money. If you're eating at Chipotle three times a week, buying dumb stuff on Amazon, and going to Disneyland whenever you want (even though you know you can't afford it), you'll be stuck playing that game for the rest of your life. Your frivolous spending will increase along *with* your income and you'll always feel two steps behind, even when you're making $100,000 a year.

But, if you trim the fat, cut your expenses down to the bare minimum, live as cheaply as possible for awhile, save some money, and really think about what you spend your money on, you'll have a much better handle on your financial life. As your income increases (and it will) you'll be smarter about how you spend your money because in the beginning you had to be.

So enjoy this difficult, frustrating, brand new, scary, awesome time. It'll be gone before you know it. The good news is Top Ramen® will always be cheap.

Are You Ready?

I've put together a foolproof flowchart that will tell you if you're ready to be a full-time musician. (Disclaimer: this is definitely not foolproof.)

ARE YOU READY TO BE A
FULL TIME MUSICIAN?

ARE YOU MAKING AT LEAST **SOME** MONEY BEING A MUSICIAN?

YES

DO YOU HAVE ENOUGH MONEY TO COVER YOUR **MONTHLY EXPENSES?**

NO

YES

NO

YOU'RE NOT QUITE READY

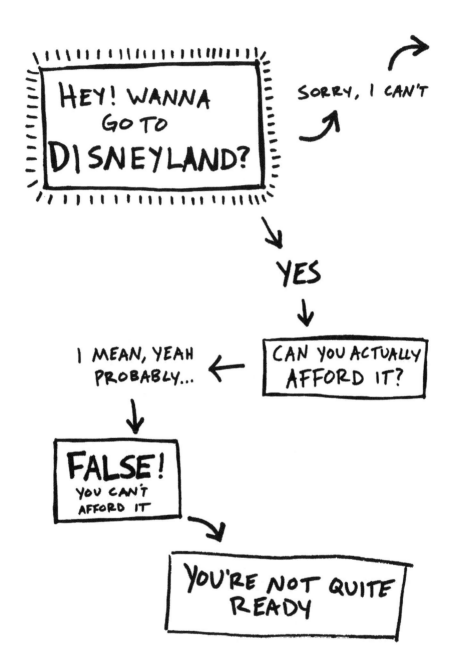

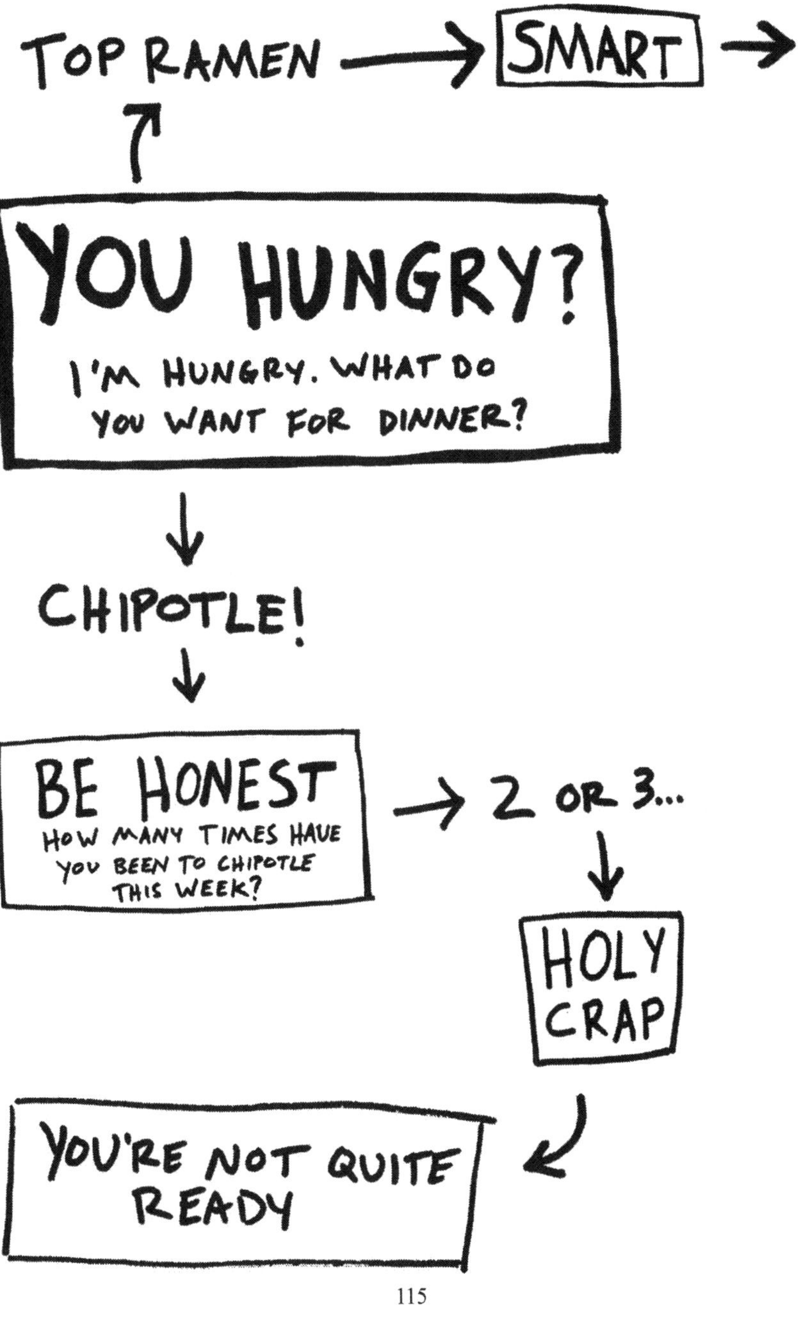

TOP RAMEN ⟶ SMART →

YOU HUNGRY?
I'M HUNGRY. WHAT DO
YOU WANT FOR DINNER?

↑ (arrow to TOP RAMEN)

↓

CHIPOTLE!

↓

BE HONEST
HOW MANY TIMES HAVE
YOU BEEN TO CHIPOTLE
THIS WEEK?

→ 2 OR 3...

↓

HOLY CRAP

↙

YOU'RE NOT QUITE READY

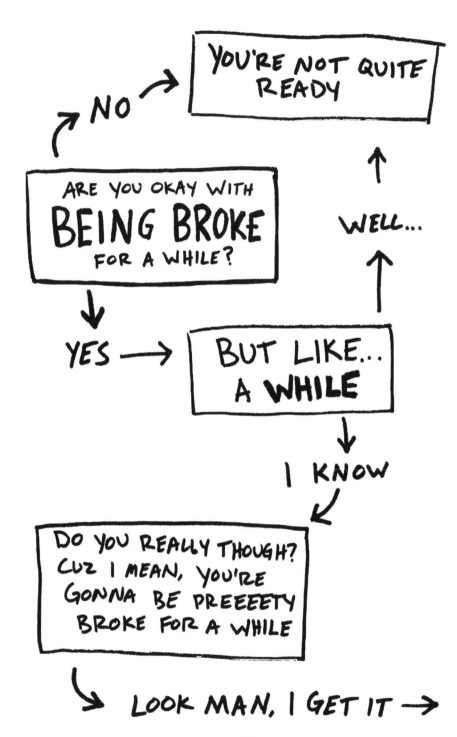

So, are you ready to take the plunge and become a full-time musician?

If your numbers add up, your runway is set, and you really know what you're getting into, then yes, you're ready! If not, that's okay, you'll get there. Keep working hard and don't get discouraged. You're building a business, remember?

In the meantime, my brother's Netflix password is "iH8UBR4ND0N". Good luck!

CHAPTER 13
MUSIC DIRECTION
& FAMILY LIFE
W/ZACH RUDULPH

Photo: Juliann Cheryl

Entering Zach Rudulph's garage, I see a ladder and hovering above it, a pair of legs disappearing into the ceiling. "Hey man, can you toss me that case right there?" shouts Zach from above. His hand appears and points to a MONO case next to me. I weave around the motorcycle and past a stuffed Iron Man, grab the case and hand it to him, still unable to see anything but his legs. I hand up a few more things before Zach descends and folds up the ladder. "Hey man! Sorry, just cleaning up, these kids man..."

Zach Rudulph is a monster musician. He's played bass with artists like Cody Simpson, Colbie Caillat, Fifth Harmony, and Gavin DeGraw, and he's currently the bass player and musical director for Andy Grammer. He tours all over the world, plays for hundreds of thousands of people, and doesn't plan on stopping any time soon.

But Zach isn't just a great musician, he's the type of person who amps up the positivity just by entering a room. He looks like Drake with dreads, has a very Denzel voice, and is one of the most genuine people I've met. If you listen to the *Startup Musician* podcast, you've heard from Zach before (episode 12), but this interview gave me a deeper understanding of what Zach does, how he does it, and *why*.

# # #

What kinds of things make up your job?

It varies, which I actually kind of like. It's not a typical nine-to-five, but it usually involves coming up with the setlist, running it by the boss [Andy Grammer], and making sure the band is ready to play.

As the music director, my job is making sure that the band doesn't suck; making sure that when Andy plays, he's not concerned with how the drums are playing the groove, or if the guitar part is right. He'll notice if something doesn't sound right and my job is to try and suss all that out before Andy even hits the stage so that he can just play.

I'm in charge of hitting stop and go on the backing tracks. We've broken out some of the delegation now, which is nice. I still have my hands in it, but we have someone who's really good with the technical side. I used to do all of that, but we've separated that out and it's been really helpful. When we need new sounds we used to have to go to the producer and ask for specific sounds for the background tracks and it was always hard. Now we have another guy who stays home and he has all the tracks. If we need them he'll send them out. We also have them on Dropbox now so we can just pull them down if we need them.

Running backing tracks used to be something that I didn't understand. I like if you were running tracks, you were halfway to being Milli Vanilli, the 100% the worst thing you could ever be. However, current pop music has so much production, so many layers, and so many sounds that aren't made with natural instruments, that tracks are now an essential part of any live show.

With Andy we'll be halfway through a tour and he'll say, "Let's cut out that whole verse," or "Let's put a stop here," or we'll come up with something as we're playing and we'll pause as a band, and I'll go back in the tracks and cut that out. I'll do simple editing along the way, but if it's heavy stuff, we try to do that before, or I'll send it to one of the guys on the team for quick edits and maybe rearrangements, or shortened intros.

Actually I just did that with ProTools[16] to change the pitch of the horns. I had real horns recorded and then we decided it needed to be shorter so I re-pitched them and edited it and hey! New intro! We actually have to learn it for this weekend because this is the new intro.

Everything Zach has mentioned so far falls under his music director duties, the behind the scenes prep work that goes into making

---

[16] Pro Tools is an audio editing product of Avid.

Andy Grammer's live show. This doesn't include his other, more visible job of being the band's bass player.

Playing bass is its own thing. Just play the bass part right, that's my job; electric and key bass. When we were a smaller unit I played an upright. I don't know if we'll go back to that again unless it's a very intentional "stripped down" version. That's a bit of a bummer because I don't get to play upright that much anymore.

What is one thing you are particularly good at?

Other people say that as an MD, I'm good at seeing the whole vision. I can see ahead and think, "This song is going to go good with this, and then we'll make this transition like this, and then we're going to do these dance moves," (which I choreograph too) and that's nice for Andy because he just trusts me now. He's the one who said I'm good seeing the whole vision.

I'm good at being a leader. I have been leading other stuff in life for a long time, small things, big things, missions trips out of the country, leading with worship teams around church. Since I was a kid I led the little band we had so it does feel natural. It's not awkward, it doesn't make me nervous, it just feels like that's what I'm supposed to do.

What does an average workweek look like for you?

I feel like I have an A life, a B life, and a C life. A is bus life, B is flight life, and C is home life.

In my life *right now*, the most consistent thing is being on a tour bus, which sounds crazy, you have a somewhat predictable schedule with gaps of time that you can usually count on. I'm going to wake up at this time. I'm probably going to go to bed at this time. I'm going to get this much sleep, then I'm going to have this block in my day to do whatever I want. I actually get more practicing done on the tour bus then anywhere else right now.

Flight life is the hardest because you get up early, you drive all the way to LAX, which adds a couple of hours, you go through security, you do the whole thing. You get to wherever you're going and you usually just go straight to bed. Then you get up and have sound check so that day just goes by. Then after the show they want to get us home, so we leave for the airport at the crack of dawn to get back to LA. I might have two or three days, maybe four days, before we fly out again. Right now it's like four days on, three days off for the next three months so I just let it be and come home in between. That's kind of how the B life goes.

C is when I know I'm going to be home for a chunk of time, like two months, which hasn't happened in a while. Then I reorganize my garage, get back to self-discipline, I love exercising, and dive back in to Dad life. I haven't had C life in a while.

Maintaining Zach's schedule is no easy feat. On any given day he can be on a bus, a plane, a stage, or at home with his wife and two sons both under the age of five. I can't imagine the mental energy it takes to switch between modes A, B, and C.

As I've gotten older I've learned to be a little easier on myself if I didn't get to this or if I didn't get to do anything musical, or whatever. That's life. It also makes the time that I do practice more meaningful.

When you're home, how does a typical day break down for you?

Mondays usually involve Daddy Day Care for sure. That's like "my day." Tuesday, Wednesday, and Thursday, we have a sitter, but on Tuesday they're here, so they're rapping on the garage like, "Let me in!" and I'm keeping them at bay.

(Cue faint cry of a four year old from the other room.) I try to hide in the garage, but they know where I'm at. Wednesday the boys are here but with other friends so they're very occupied. Thursday is my most productive day because they go to the other kids' home.

On Friday I'm usually leaving but if I'm home, my wife and I share the responsibility of the boys together because she has a half-day on Friday. Lately if I'm home on the weekend I get to do a couple of cover gigs sometimes, which I enjoy, and then play at my church on Sunday. And that's how it works.

Balancing a career, especially in music, while also raising children is a challenge. I'm exhausted just thinking about Zach's schedule, but he's been able to make the touring, the playing, and the music directing work, all while being involved in his children's lives.

What does your actual "work" look like?

As music director, I've gotten better at Ableton, mainly because it's been a super solid platform for playback. I trigger the tracks from a Launchpad. In an ideal world, if you've done production ahead of time, you don't need to change anything. The Ableton session is there as a playback device. It's so simple; the learning curve was really low.

I had to get better at understanding the signal path for our track world. We're running two computers at the same time, so that means whatever I edit on this computer, I have to copy it over to the other computer too, so I also keep everything on a hard drive. Everything is basically in three places. Both computers are playing at the same time; you just only hear one. If that one messes up, it immediately switches to the other computer. These are things I've had to wrap my head around.

When I'm home, I'm always trying to get better. I feel

like the good music directors, they're really good at a chorded instrument like guitar or piano. I'm trying to get better at piano, just to be able to chunk out chords. I have a fun book I found.

Zach pulls out a book and geeks out about the 7 chords, 2, 5, 1's. Then he dives into his complete practice routine, pulls out his looper pedal, plays some exercises, and basically gives me a private concert.

With producing, for me, it's about practicing the whole process. So that means coming up with beats, or grooves, or whatever, and recording it to see what happens. I recently produced something and gave it to Andy. He's in writing mode for the next album and he's totally down to take anybody's stuff. He'd rather keep it all in the family if he can as far as writing goes. He's an amazing writer himself, but he's always down for chord change ideas or rough drafts. I like that. I'm not good enough at producing to make it sonically, scientifically sound. I can't deliver a complete package; I haven't practiced producing enough. But I could probably come up with something that you could run with.

I feel like I have enough musical knowledge, but I'm a little behind the curve on how to get that out. I want to continue to use ProTools and I just recently paid about a grand to split the cost of the Kontact Complete program with a friend. I have no excuses now. Well, I need a new computer to run it right…

Even with a successful career, Zach is still eager to learn. Whether it's piano, producing, or getting better at software tools, he continuously works to increase the value of his startup.

Do you have any sort of regular schedule or routines?

When I'm on the bus, I work out, that's "me time." When I'm at home, if I can get in three days, I'm happy, I'm mentally stable. Otherwise I'll lose my mind. Yesterday it was

125

7 o'clock at night. Tomorrow I hope it'll be in the morning. Probably not going to do it today and that's okay. That's another thing I've accepted as I've gotten older, I used to be bigger, stronger, more athletic, but I'm okay with that.

At home, I'm chasing the boys around and that throws me off because I like the discipline of life, but I've learned to just squeeze things in. If they happen to take a nap at the same time, I'll pull out my bass and play something after I've cleaned up whatever's going on.

It's hard because mentally I'm in a place where I want to practice producing and I want to practice the bass and sometimes I just can't because of "baby life." But that's fine. It's basically whenever I can, like working out, whenever I can. I think once they start going to school, then I'll be able to force myself to get back into something and have no other excuses.

Do you have any non-music hobbies?

Exercise; that's my go to non-music hobby, and riding my motorcycle. I have one but I don't get to ride that much.

What is your life like outside of music?

I've been married for 10 years. I have a four year old, and a one and a half year old. They're awesome. The garage is where I try to run away, I'm trying to get some carpet to make it feel even warmer and home like.

The garage is a snapshot of Zach's life. There's his motorcycle next to a shelf full of bass amps, stands, and cables. His desk is functional with a computer monitor, keyboard, and iPad. The piano directly to the right is plugged into the speakers for easy access. On the wall across from us hang pictures of Zach and his wife, Diana and there's a stuffed Iron Man on the floor.

What is the hardest part about being a freelance musician?

Social media, because age wise I'm just over the cusp of social media. But it's such a vital thing you have to be doing with any career in this era. The last thing I want to do is go post something, especially when I'm traveling and touring. That was an area that was lacking for me, but the only way people know you're still doing what you're doing is through social media, so it has to be up to par. I found a friend of mine who loves it to do it for me. This is like a grown-up use of my money. Juliann is awesome and now she helps with that.

Making sure your promotions are always up to par is another part that I don't like doing. Making sure your website is decent and usable. Making sure you stay relevant. Did you put a photo up recently? Are you playing an instrument in that photo? Juliann helps me keep on it. I also have a couple of companies that I love and some endorsements so Juliann is also cool about letting them know what I'm up to, which is good because I often forget. We just did Today [on NBC] last Friday and Juliann was pivotal in giving those companies a heads up.

The digital world is like a parallel life. If you're not somewhat active online, for some audiences, you don't exist. For Zach, the solution was to hire it out. For you, that means posting something other than a cat video every now and then.

If you could play one show with one artist, dead or alive, who would it be?

I have to go with Earth Wind & Fire. That's my favorite band. Everything about their songwriting, everything about their party atmosphere, everybody up and going, it's literally how I think our show is with Andy Grammer. We try to be infectious, and to me, anything Earth Wind & Fire did is infectious. You want to be in on it.

Do I want to be Verdine White? I don't know. But if you went to an Earth Wind & Fire show and he wasn't there, it wouldn't be the same. I want to be that way. I think one of the things I excel at is just being me. If I play on a project usually they're like, "We want you back for you!" Andy doesn't even want to do a show without me because he's like, "My show's not the same." Just like if Verdine White wasn't there. He's gotta be there, dancing around, you know?

For a musician, the job is about more than how well you can play; it's also about who you are as a person. When you are on tour, you play the show for two hours a night, but what about the other 22 hours in the day? Those are the hours you spend with the band, hanging out and living life. If you're a terrible person to be around, they probably won't let you on the bus.

Zach is someone you want on your bus. He's mastered the art of being a great musician and music director, but he's not going to settle for where he's at. He's always striving for more; learning new things, making the show better, and adding incredible value to his startup.

CHAPTER 14
MAKING CONNECTIONS

You Should Be Talking

During my sophomore year of college I was sitting in an 8:20 a.m. music class waiting for the professor to arrive. It was silent, partly because it was early but also because no one really knew each other. I was sitting in a corner by myself (not in a "Nobody likes me," kind of way, but more like "It's early, I don't know you, please don't talk to me,").

When the professor walked in he broke the silence with a loud, "Why isn't anyone talking?!" More silence. "You guys should be talking! Why aren't you talking?!" he asked.

While his question initially seemed sarcastic, after a moment it became clear that he actually wanted us to be talking. This felt strange, especially since in literally every other classroom I'd been in, the teacher wanted us to stop talking when they entered the room.

After another minute of silence, the professor said, "Look, you guys should be talking. You should get to know each other. As soon as you get out of school, who do you think is going to call you for work? The people in this room, the people you're in school with."

It took some time, but over the next few weeks, people began to open up and talk to each other, even at 8:20 a.m.

You Have to Network to Get Work

You've probably heard someone say, "It's not *what* you know, it's *who* you know" and this is absolutely true. The most important thing you can do to get more work is to get to know more people. This is known as "networking."

I hate that word.

Maybe it's because it's so heavily associated with the business world, but for me, networking just has an air of douchiness about it. I picture a sleazy guy in a cheap suit schmoozing the biggest name in the room, solely because he wants more work. He pours on the pseudo-friendliness to get what he wants.

"Hey what's up man, you sound great, my name's Tevin, you play a lot of straight ahead stuff? Nice, nice. I'd love to sit in some time, when I'm not on the road, you know? Cool, cool."

Tevin is a textbook douche. Nobody likes Tevin.

What Networking Isn't

Networking is not self-promotion. It's not telling people that you play guitar too, and probably better than the guy they currently have, and they just *have* to hear you play.

Networking is not about climbing to the top of somebody's call list as soon as possible. It's not about beating other musicians to the punch.

Networking is not social media blather. It's not a braggy "Today's Office" image or a #blessed post.

To be honest, networking isn't about you at all. Don't promote yourself. That will come up eventually anyway. Ask the other person about himself or herself, and if there's something about yourself that's actually relevant, then bring it up.

What Networking Is

Networking at its simplest form is getting to know other people. This isn't to say you should just inflate their ego and make them feel good about themselves, but focus on the person you're trying to get to know. Ask them questions, let them talk, and really get to know them.

In many professions there's a general rule that you shouldn't be friends with your employees. In the world of professional musicians, it's exactly the opposite. Musicians want to be employees with their friends. Who calls musicians for work? Other musicians. Why did they call a particular person? Because they *know* them, not because they googled "drummer" and hit "I'm feeling lucky."

Networking in Action

Let's flip this around. Instead of talking about what you should and shouldn't do, let's think about what you would and wouldn't like done to you.

Scenario 1: You've just finished playing a gig, you're worn out, and it's late. A young kid with lots of energy comes up to you and says, "Hey man I play drums. My name's Tevin."

Your immediate thought is going to be, "Ok cool, and thanks for that, Tevin." Your second thought is going to be, "What kind of name is Tevin?"

He continues to tell you how he took a lesson with Vinnie once and forces a business card on you. You don't give him a business card in return because then he's going to actually call you and continue this conversation.

You say, "Nice to meet you," and he finishes with, "I play jazz, classical, pop, Latin, and robo-core." You say goodbye and promptly throw his business card in the trash.

Dammit Tevin, you're the worst. Don't be like Tevin!

What Tevin Should Have Done...

Scenario 2: You just finished playing a gig, you're worn out, and it's late. A young kid comes up to you and says, "Great job, you guys sounded fantastic. What was the name of that last song?"

You reply, "Thanks, it was 'Smooth.'"

The kid responds, "Ahh, I thought I recognized it, I love *anything* featuring Rob Thomas. I'm so glad I got to come see you guys tonight."

The conversation continues and it turns out this kid really knows his Rob Thomas, not to mention Santana. You finally wrap it up and ask, "Great talking to you, what was your name?"

"Kevin Sebastian Brockroth."

Now you guys have had a conversation. Now you're going to remember his name. The next time you run into him, you'll actually want to talk to him.

Nicely done, Kevin.

What Kevin Did Right...

Notice that in this scenario Kevin didn't force his business card on you, but you actually wouldn't mind talking to him again. Kevin may not give you his card at your first meeting, your second, or even your third, but as you guys get to know each other, it'll come up. Let it happen.

Also, notice that Kevin didn't talk about himself. Networking is hanging out with people and getting to know them, not in an artificial way to gain gigs, but to actually get to know the person.

Building Friendships

There's a big different between using people to get what you want and building genuine friendships. When you get to play with a great musician who is also a friend, you look forward to it all month. Not just for the music, but for the hang.

Maybe the friend gets you gigs, maybe he doesn't. But you don't even care about that. Hanging out with the friend is its own reward. You two don't brag to each other, don't falsely compliment each other, and don't try to "network" each other. You're friends first, musicians second.

The friend is a great musician, gigs frequently, and is a blast to hang out with. He may not be attacking the networking scene like Tevin, but in 10 years he'll have a strong career, built with the help of people who love working with him.

Are You a Tevin or a Friend? (Take this Quick Quiz to Find Out)

• Tevin wants people to call him for gigs. A friend wants people to call him to hang out.

• Tevin wants ALL OF THE GIGS, RIGHT NOW. A friend wants to play great music with great people who love music.

• Tevin is focused on "networking." A friend is focused on cultivating relationships.

• Tevin wants you to call him for gigs. Did I mention that?

Look, let's be real. We all want to be called for gigs. That's what we're trying to do here. But Tevin's method of douchily (it's a word) trying to get gigs is not the way to do it.

To be fair, his strategy technically works. He does play a lot of gigs (did you hear he played on Kimmel?) but his aggressive networking techniques and tendency to use people on his way to the top will eventually catch up to him. In 10 years he'll be the jaded musician who complains after your gig about how he used to tour the world, but the music industry has changed and he got screwed.

A friend, on the other hand, may not have as many gigs right now, but he has plenty of people who genuinely care about his success. The friendships that he is building will not only help him through the next 10 years, but for the rest of his life. Rather than using other people to climb to the top, he's climbing the ladder with other people.

If you want to build a successful career as a professional musician, stop "networking" and focus on making connections and building friendships. Not fake friendships with secret selfish motives. Not friendships so you check a box that says, "we're friends." I'm talking about genuine, honest, real friendships.

Musicians want to work with their friends so the career aspect of it will take care of itself. If you want to get more work, go make more friends. Before long you'll have lifelong friends, a solid career foundation, and you'll also "Get them gigs, Bruh!" in the process.

Great Idea, Brandon! How Would I Go About Doing That?

There's a whole world of people out there who aren't Tevin, but aren't quite your friend. So let's up our networking friendship game.

Here's a homework assignment for you:

- Text two people that you haven't seen in a while.

- Set up some time next week to get together; lunch, coffee, drinks, or just hanging out.

- Go into it with no end goal in mind other than hanging out with a friend. Don't try to get a gig out of this interaction.

- Ask the other person good questions about what they're up to. Don't talk about yourself unless they ask. Just go be a good friend to someone.

Other Networking Opportunities

Obviously, there are a lot of different scenarios that could play out here. Rather than script out every single one, let's talk about a few other ways to expand your network.

Networking at a Gig

How to do you make a connection when you've just seen someone play, but you haven't played yourself? This can be a tricky scenario because they've established themselves as a good musician, and you're just some guy.

Don't be overly pushy or they'll ignore you. Don't force your card on them or talk about yourself unless it's something relevant. "Oh Kevin? Yeah, I love that guy, it's always great playing with him." It may take multiple interactions to get to know the other person and be comfortable enough to exchange information. Be patient, grasshopper.

It's much easier to make that connection when you are both playing. This is a good situation because you get a feel for how they play, and they get a feel for how you play. On the breaks between playing, get to know them, and at the end of the gig, if it feels right ask, "Hey can I get your info?"

This is the ideal scenario since they've both heard you play and have a feeling for who you are as a person. So during the break, DO NOT get on your phone. Instead, talk to the people you're playing with. This is the ideal time to get to know them.

Networking in Your League

While we're still on our Tevin kick, let's talk about something else he *loves* to do. Tevin is always talking about big name musicians. And he's trying to network the hell of out them.

For a long time I used to play this game too. You see other musicians that seem to be at a higher level; like, a *much* higher level. I'm talking the *bass player from Coldplay* status. You want to be there too, so you try to hang out with them, try to win their approval. Nothing would mean more to you than a "You sounded good" from them. (Because obviously a "You sounded good" leads to "Can I get your number?" which leads to "Are you available for this gig?" which leads to you replacing the current bass player from Coldplay, and being besties for life. Slap a mid-air high five, FREEZE FRAME, roll credits.)

I'm now officially the new "Bass Player from Coldplay!"

It's great to have musical idols and people you look up to. You absolutely should. If I saw Steve Jordan on the street I would definitely need to change my pants in response to the groove he was playing (don't ask).

But here's the thing. Steve Jordan is NEVER going to call me to play with him. Never. Not now, not next week, not in 10 years, not ever. Why? Because he plays with Pino Palladino and 100 other amazing bassists and I'm just some guy on the street who smells like soiled pants.

I can try my hardest to network Steve Jordan, hit him up for coffee, and retweet everything he says, but it's still not going to happen. He's got his list of bass players he loves to play with, and at least 100 other guys also trying to network him to death. And while I'm busy trying to get Steve to notice me, my peers are off working. They're making great music, doing new and unique things, growing their own startups. Or maybe they're playing in the worst dive bar ever from 9 p.m. to 1:30 a.m. for $70. Either way, they're out there doing things and growing their network.

So, instead of focusing on the musicians a level or two above you, focus on the musicians at your *current* level. There's a ton of talent there too. These are the people who *are* going to call you tomorrow, next week, and in 10 years for gigs. Focus on getting to know them and making great music with them. This week it may be stupid bar gigs for $70, but who knows, in a few years you could be playing with the same musicians for a lot more money.

Now that I've been out of school for several years, musicians that I went to school with are doing some really cool things. They're touring the world with artists like Andy Grammer, Idina Menzel, and Eric Hutchinson. They're teaching at colleges and universities. They're playing private events every single weekend. They're building recording studios, starting companies, releasing records, and creating amazing music, and making a living doing what they love to do.

Because I came up with them, I've had an opportunity to tag along for the ride. I've been able to record some great music, play some amazing venues, travel the world, and work with some fantastic musicians; all things I would have missed if I were trying to network up like Tevin.

When the people on your level achieve great things, they bring people up with them. When you achieve great things, you bring those around you along for the ride. And as you move up, you'll get to work with more and more excellent musicians who you never thought you'd meet let alone work with. And maybe, just maybe, one of those people will be Steve Jordan. In this scenario though, it is years later, and I've obviously changed my pants.

Networking with "The Enemy"

The other people who play your instrument are not the enemy. This isn't *The Hunger Games*. If you take a "you versus everyone else out there that plays your instrument" approach, you'll start to alienate yourself and other people won't want to work with you. Also, you'll drive yourself crazy.

Think of your fellow musician as a friend who is trying to make a living just like you (because, spoiler alert, that's exactly what they are). By being supportive and sticking together, you can both win, without having to kill each other in the process.

Okay, but why?

Why is "internal" networking important? Why should you befriend the people with whom you are technically competing for gigs? Why should you "volunteer as tribute?" Because when you get to know the people who might "steal" your gigs, and give them work, you'll get more work in the process.

If you're a drummer, unless you're playing in a STOMP style group, chances are you won't play a lot of gigs with other drummers. A drummer isn't going to call another drummer to play together at a gig, but they *will* call the other drummer to sub for them when they can't make it.

Who are they going to call? No, still not *Ghostbusters*, sorry. They're going to call someone who they know is a good player and a good person. They may not be playing the gig, but it's still their reputation on the line. If you're friends with other people playing your instrument, taking sub gigs is a great way to expand your network and get more work.

You need to be the best sub anyone could ask for. There are a few reasons why this is a good idea:

- In the short term: You'll make money. You'll walk away at the end of the night with $100 in your pocket. A gig's a gig's a gig.

- In the slightly longer term: The person you subbed for will call you for more sub gigs. At some point, they're not going to be able to make it to another gig. If you killed it as a sub in the past, you'll be at the top of their call list.

- In the long term: You're expanding your network and playing with musicians you wouldn't otherwise play with. All of a sudden, there's a whole new crew of people who know you and your playing. If the person you subbed for has to miss a gig again, you're at the top of a whole bunch of other lists. And if they permanently can't do it, you'll be the new regular guy.

Speaking from experience, subbing can generate a lot of work. Not only from one-off gigs, but from permanently taking over the reoccurring gig for friends of mine. I've also been able to give my friends one-off and permanent work when I'm unavailable.

Your fellow guitarists/drummers/singers/[insert your specialty here] are *not* your enemy. View them as friends and you'll get more work then you know what to do with. You'll have a great sub list to call when *you* can't make it. Don't try to kill each other, you won't win by doing that. Get to know them, hang out together, and hey, maybe watch *The Hunger*

Games movies if you somehow missed them.

Be Good

Who you are is just as important as how you play. Musicians want to surround themselves with people that they like. Nobody likes playing with the guy who sounds great but thinks he's better than everyone else. So be kind and be good to people. Help people out when they're in need. Be fun to be around. Be genuine.

If you're a great musician and you're genuinely good to people, you'll have more work than you know what to do with. You may even have to sub some of it out. My name's Tevin by the way, I play drums, and I'll totally sub for you.

CHAPTER 15
COMPOSITION &
CREATING CONNECTIONS
W/ ZACH MARSH

Photo: Sean Sidders

When you head down the Startup Musician path, you're launching a business and you're going to have to hustle to see your startup to succeed. You have to think like an entrepreneur, not an employee. Employees do what they're told. Entrepreneurs are always searching for creative ways to get what they want.

Enter Zach Marsh. He looks like a hipster, but he was dressing this way long before hipster fashion was a thing. He fully embraces the Birkenstocks, the footwear of his homeland, and isn't afraid to laugh at himself.

Zach is a composer, pianist, and teacher, and one of the most entrepreneurial musicians I've ever met. We sat down in his apartment in South Pasadena, California, to discuss his career and his creative thinking.

♯ ♯ ♯

What types of things have you composed music for?

The *coolest* things that I've done…I wrote some extra jazz cues for *Daredevil*, the TV show on Netflix and I'm currently writing some additional music for *VeggieTales* on Netflix, which is super fun and sometimes obnoxious. Last year I did some cues for a film called *Same Kind of Different as Me*, which had Greg Kinnear and Renée Zellweger in it. It was just a few jazz cues *very* far in the background. And then on a daily basis I do a lot of web videos and short films. I'm working on a feature film right now that's kind of an action-thriller thing.

Is it the next Terminator movie?!

No, it's low budget, *very* low budget, but it's fun. The music is really minimal electronic, very gritty stuff.

What about piano playing? Where are you at with that?

I don't play that often anymore because I do a lot more production work now, but when I am playing, I play with a jazz combo out of Burbank and for our church and I do a lot of one-time gigs with random people. I'm working with an artist now and he's very soul, and R&B. I usually do soul, R&B, a little bit of hip hop, and jazz.

How does teaching fit into this plan?

I teach at an after-school program for kids with autism called The Miracle Project and we create original musicals. We meet once a week and write the music with the students for a 40-minute show and then they perform the show at the end of the year. Last year we did three different classes at the same time and we wrote a different show for each one. Each show had about six songs. They're all kid songs and they're super fun.

Zach reaches over to his and plays a song that he wrote with the kids.

"We can't wait to get to Dance Island,
We've been sailing for days to get to Dance Island,
We've been dreaming of ways to get to Dance Island,
And it's finally the day we get to Dance Island."

And it's exactly the type of song you might expect from a man who also writes music for animated singing vegetables.

Working with the kids is super fun and it's been a huge outlet for me because I get to create really silly things with them. We have a whole rap number that incorporates the latest dance moves. Being able to work with these kids has just been amazing. I studied music therapy for two years and I'm very interested in how music can literally change the way the brain perceives and processes things. I get to experiment with that and see the practical application of it through this program.

Between the composing, the performing, and the teaching, what do you feel is the one thing that you're particularly good at?

With composing, I've been moving into the music library world. I sent in all of this stuff that I'm really proud of and one was a *VeggieTales* reel. It was mixed in there with all of this more heavy and serious music that I was doing and they're all, "We really like this *VeggieTales* music! We could really use more of that in our library." It made me think, that's what I do naturally, and I do it well. That silly dopey stuff, I could do that all day.

What does the term "music library" actually mean?

It's a newer thing for me too, something that I'm just getting into. When I looked at getting into composition, I *thought* composition was this: you get hired for a project, they send you a video and you write the music for it. That's definitely being a film composer or a composer for any type of visual media, but music libraries are just tracks. You're just submitting tracks to an aggregate and then they try to place those tracks with TV or whatever type of web thing. And their clients can also go into the music library and audition the tracks that you're submitting.

As opposed to a custom tailored score?

Yeah. This is the model that a lot of things are shifting towards, especially with the amount of content being produced. YouTube people are publishing high quality videos hourly, minutely, and YouTube has a different sync license than maybe TV does. So if you buy a song for TV it's gonna be a higher fee but if you buy it for YouTube it'll be cheaper. I think it's a single use fee. There are a bunch of tiers. There are tons of different music libraries. There's the "big box store" type of music library, and their whole thing is having thousands and thousands of tracks that are cheaper and not as high in quality. It's easier to get tracks into these because they release something like 500 tracks a month.

But the other one I'm writing for is like a "boutique" music library and they release them like "I'm gonna be an artist." So, "I am Zach Marsh, the artist. Here is my photo and here is my EP of songs. This is my thing, this is what I do." They'll probably say "family adventure," that's a title they use a lot, or "happy orchestra," something like that. So that'll be my bend to them. This is a new way of looking things for me, that I can market myself to them as "The *VeggieTales* guy."

As a composer, I'm going to write good tracks, and for higher quality libraries, I'm definitely going to spend more time on them. But for lower quality ones, I'm just going to pump out tracks. For the library that sends out 500 tracks per month, if I can submit 100 tracks to them that's great. Over 10 months they'll maybe submit 10 of mine. If you can have this big pool of songs that people are licensing every few days for $20, even though it's not a lot of money, it starts to accumulate. That's the business model.

What I appreciate about Zach is his ability to see value in the small things as well as the big things. While he's worked on some larger composition projects, he's also worked on many more small projects. These are the less glamorous ones; the projects you probably haven't heard about, or even realized that the music needed to be licensed. Zach's ability to see value in both types of projects serves him well.

What does an average week of work look like for you?

I'm just going to give you this week because it *is* so varying. One of the main things for me is that when I have a lot of work my week looks awesome, and when I don't have a lot of work it's really hard for me to do the things that I know

I should be doing. I'm sure you can relate.

Yup! This phenomenon is called Parkinson's Law, which says that work will expand to fill the time allotted. I've found this to be completely true. If I have one thing to do and I have all day to do it, I'm not going to do it until 3 a.m. But if I have 10 things to do, I'm going to get all 10 things done by noon.

That's going to be the test with these music libraries because there isn't really a deadline, you submit when you're ready you go. I'm getting married in two weeks so I have a very firm deadline. By next Friday I have to have all the tracks in for the film so I've got to get those all done and hopefully make a dent in some of these music library tracks before I fly out to Seattle.

I work out Mondays, Wednesdays, and Fridays and that's been really helpful for me in terms of consistency in my life. I go to this place in Burbank, and then I come back, eat lunch, and then I'm usually working. This week I was working on the feature film on Monday and then around 3 p.m. I go to Santa Monica where I teach. Lately I've been doing wedding stuff in the evenings.

Tuesday I met with an artist in the morning; we were collaborating for an album. I was supposed to meet with another artist but that got pushed back. More work on the film.

Wednesday, work out and then I go to a homeless ministry in the afternoons and then usually church practice in the evening if I'm scheduled that week. If not, I'm usually here or hanging out with my fiancé. On Wednesday I also had a meeting with a guy who works for a trailer company. I was getting to know him and submitting some of my work for him.

Today (Thursday) I had a meeting with an app company that I'm currently promoting on my YouTube channel. They pay me monthly to promote their app and we're working on an ad segment that will play before my video. Right now we're doing this interview and then this afternoon I teach and I'll be working on getting this short film. They just gave me the final picture lock so I have to move some things around. They liked all the music except one cue that I need to redo. Tomorrow I'm meeting with the music library guy.

I played a gig this weekend and have another gig coming up next weekend. I'm doing maybe two to three gigs a month, plus church, and the music libraries, and YouTube.

Zach's YouTube channel has a unique origin story. A few years ago Zach answered an ad on Craigslist advertising for someone to make easy piano tutorial videos for pop songs for $25 per video. Zach would make the videos, the Craigslist guy (whom we'll just call "Craig") would upload the videos to his YouTube channel, and Zach would receive $25. After a while, Craig (whom Zach has never met in person) decided to close down the channel. Being the creative thinker he is, Zach convinced Craig to give him the channel. Today, Zach's YouTube channel, Pianoitall, has over 150 videos and more than 170,000 subscribers. Zach has also managed to monetize his YouTube channel in multiple ways; YouTube now pays half his rent!

Zach geeks out for 10 more minutes explaining how it all works; the ins and outs of how he makes his tutorial videos, uploads them, tags them, enables YouTube ads, and then offers a free sheet music download on his own external website, which also serves ads. (To read this portion of the interview would be torture, but the video of this entire interview is available at www.startupmusician.co/bookbonus.)

What is your personal life like?

After we get married, we're going to live here in South Pasadena in a two-bedroom apartment. So yes, you *can* be married and be a full-time musician. My fiancé, Rachel, works in marketing so she has a little bit more of a stable job, which is nice. I think I do have some fears about making sure that I'm always holding up my end of the deal but it's worked out. I'm always working is basically how it is.

What is the hardest part about being a freelance musician?

Uncertainty. Not knowing what next month will look like, if next month is going to have nothing and this month has everything all in one. So I have to be more of a planner, which is especially hard for me in terms of finances. Being able to plan for the slower months and figure out what are you going to do in those months that's productive and not just cry yourself to sleep.

One of the things that I think is hard, especially for composers to figure out, is that free work is a good thing. Doing stuff for free is good, within reason. You have to be careful, but a lot of guys I know, even those who are high up and working on bigger budget stuff, will still do stuff for free every once in awhile. There is no bad exposure. A lot of the things that I'm doing now came from really small or even no budget stuff that's grown into bigger things.

The work that I do with the afterschool program started for $25 an hour for two hours a week. So $50 bucks a week two years ago is now the majority of my income through negotiating and through more work. It's the same thing with the YouTube channel; it also started with $25. People would laugh at $25 gigs like, "I'm not gonna ever work for that!" but you start from there and then think, "How can I make this bigger? How I can I make this into something I can do long term?" It's the same thing with a lot of score work. I work with a company called Roadtrippers and I think the first video I did was for $200. But now it's $500 for a two-minute video.

What is a creative way to get more composition work?

I'll give you all my secrets. Some friends gave them to me so I'm going pass them on. Go onto Vimeo, Kickstarter, Instagram, maybe Snapchat (I don't know, I don't use Snapchat). But go onto those platforms and find somebody that you think is cool and be like, "Hey man, I do composer stuff and if you ever need music let me know. Kthanksbye."

Do you offer to do it for free?

No! When one guy got right back to me he was like, "Oh yeah, I need music. How much would something like that cost?" I think I did it for $200. It was a *Game of Thrones* promo video. It wasn't for *Game of Thrones*; it was a fan that made a *Game of Thrones* promo.

And now that I'm in Los Angeles it's been more through building relationships, trying to go out to coffee with people. That's what I did yesterday. It's about getting more comfortable without feeling like I'm "networking" and not feeling like, "Oh I hope at the end of this I get some sort work out of this with a handshake."

It should be more, "*You* love composition, *I* love composition, I'm sure we have enough to talk about for an hour and a half where it doesn't have to be an awkward lunch at In-N-Out." Yesterday we had a great lunch and we geeked out about composition for a while. I had no expectations, but at the end of that conversation he was like, "I would love to hear some of your music, why don't you send it over and we'll see if we can use it for something?"

You need to get out of your comfort zone and meet more people; just get to know people on a friend level and then let that naturally evolve.

Naturally, as opposed to "I want this from you"?

You can do both; it's not just one or the other. If it's really slow and there's a short film on Kickstarter with no composer on it, send the team an email! Take a look at what their budget is. If it's a $40,000 budget you can assume they *might* have $2,000 for music if you're lucky. If it's under $10,000 they probably don't have any money for music.

What does your success rate ratio look like with this approach?

People usually get back to you about 50% of the time, and of those people most of them will say, "We already have people," or "We're not looking for music." A few of them will be interested, and of those few, maybe one will come to fruition.

Sometimes I'll send an email to somebody and then a year later get back to me. They're like, "We weren't looking for a composer then, but now we're in post production and we remembered your email." I thought that was really cool because from that short contact where I talked about how passionate I was about their film, they remembered me.

It is a low success rate; everything is kind of a low success rate in these things, even when you get to the big stuff. That's just part of it. People might promise you a couple grand for something and then say, "Sorry we don't have that money." In my opinion people aren't usually *trying* to screw you, they just promise things they can't do.

What do you think is the most important thing you need to make it as a composer?

The one thing you need to succeed as a composer, or just as someone in the entertainment industry, is resilience. I've definitely seen that with a lot of composers who are successful now. They've had 10 years of really getting screwed over, or failing, or getting fired, and they just kept going. I've had my share of that with a couple projects that I was super excited about that just didn't happen. You've just got to keep being resilient and keep making it happen and eventually you'll make it.

Picking yourself up after you fail or something doesn't go as planned is essential to the life of a Startup Musician. Failure is traditionally seen as the opposite of success but failure actually isn't all that bad and it's a necessary step on the way to success. It's more like a pothole on an unpaved road. When you fall in, you're not going in the opposite direction of success; you're making your own path. What matters is how you recover. So get up and get going.

One last question: if you could score one movie from the past or in the future, what would it be?

My favorite movies growing up were the *Indiana Jones* trilogy. But I wouldn't have done it as well as John Williams did! Part of the reason I loved those movies was *because* John Williams scored them. So mine would be a cheap knockoff, "*Indiana Faux-nes*" or something like that.

I'd pay to see that.

CHAPTER 16
MYTHS &
TAXES

Money Mythology

Any time you put the words "musician" and "money" in the same sentence, people are going to get a little nervous (especially your parents if they paid for your college education). There are three basic myths about freelance musician and we're going to dispense with all of them right here, right now.

Myth #1: Musicians Are Poor

Perhaps the most perpetuated myth about musicians is that we are all "starving artists." We suffer for our art and live on a steady diet of Top Ramen® in our parents' basements. We view making money as "selling out, man!" and we wear our lifestyle on our sleeve as a badge of honor; except for rock stars, they make like $5.39 per second (at least, Taylor

Swift[17] does).

You already know this one isn't true. As a professional musician, you chose your career because you love music and you can't imagine doing anything else. And while it can be tough to get started and nobody wants to eat cheap noodles for the rest their life, being a freelance musician doesn't automatically mean you're going to be poor. Between the starving artists and the Taylor Swifts, there is a large population of financially viable professional musicians. These musicians work hard and make a decent living, all while doing what they love most.

Myth #2: Musicians Are Lazy

This one is my personal favorite. We all wake up at noon, make our Top Ramen®, and watch Netflix until it's time to go to our gig. Music isn't work; it's fun. Musicians basically get paid to have fun!

Musicians may wake up at 9 or 10 a.m., but that's because we got back from last night's gig at 3 a.m. A musician's schedule is often the opposite of a traditional work schedule, but that's because musicians generally work for non-musicians. When do most musicians teach? Afternoons and evenings after kids get out of school. When do musicians play the most gigs? Nights and weekends, when everyone else is relaxing after their work week.

Successful musicians are anything but lazy. They are entrepreneurs, constantly trying new things to figure out what works, what doesn't, and how to make themselves more valuable. Is music fun? Absolutely, but it's also a lot of hard work. If you sit around in your parents' basement watching hours and hours of Netflix, you deserve that Top Ramen®.

---

[17] Forbes. Full List: The Highest-Paid Celebrities of 2016.

Myth #3: Musicians Are Bad at Managing Money

Since we're poor and lazy, we musicians must not be very good at managing money. We'd rather spend money on cheap beer and more equipment than save for things like a car or a house. We are stuck in an endless cycle of poverty and will carry on like this until we eventually give up and get a "real" job.

Not all Startup Musicians are naturally good with money, but over time we learn how to be better because we have to. We work hard for our money and have to be very disciplined to make sure the bills get paid, we get the gear we need, and we can build up a savings account. Many professional musicians own their own homes and cars. It takes a lot of discipline, but it's the only way to avoid living paycheck to paycheck.

So what can you do about it? Here are a few tips.

How to Live on a Flexible Income

When you're a professional musician, every month is different. In December you made $6,000 but then January hit and you only made $1,000. Living a consistent lifestyle that doesn't fluctuate with your income takes discipline, but is ultimately the wisest thing to do.

There is no stress quite like the "How am I going to pay my cell phone bill this month?" stress. It's a feeling that I know well, and it's absolutely the worst. Stop living paycheck to paycheck as soon as humanly possible! If you're serious out this (and I know you are because you're voluntarily reading this book), trim your expenses to the bone and save as much money as you possibly can. Don't eat out as much, don't buy as much gear, and, God forbid, cancel your Netflix subscription.

155

Remember back in Chapter 12 when you worked out exactly how much money you needed to quit your day job?

Don't forget about that budget once you start to earn a little more. If you need a baseline of $3,000/month to get by, tuck away the extra $3,000 from December to cover the $2,000 deficit in January. Do this EVERY SINGLE MONTH until you have a nice little pile of extra cash in the bank. After you've built up a bit of a buffer (say, one or two month's expenses), then you've really got some flexible money to start a saving for long-term goals or make a more significant purchase.

How to Rent an Apartment

While we're at it, let's discuss how to make a significant purchase while living on a flexible income.

There will come a time in your life when you have to spend a lot of money on something, like renting an apartment, or getting car loan, or buying new gear. For people with traditional jobs, this is pretty straightforward. They walk into the bank, show some pay stubs, and walk out with a new car. (At least that's how I *think* it works.)

For freelancers though, it's a little more difficult. We don't have pay stubs. We have a hundred checks from various people. So how do you manage to rent an apartment, buy a car, or make other large financial purchases? Make it easy for the other person to say yes.

This illustration is for renting an apartment, but the same steps can be applied to almost any situation that requires you to verify your income.

- Print up three to four months of your bank statements. Organize them in a neat stack. Make an estimate of your average monthly income (total amount earned divided by the number of months included). It doesn't have to be your exact income from the previous month, but just an average of the past few months, or what you averaged last year.

• Write a cover letter to the apartment manager explaining that you are a professional musician and you don't have regular pay stubs. I've found that using the term "professional musician" strikes the appropriate tone, whereas "I play music and gigs and stuff" does not.

• In that letter, explain that your income varies but that you make an average of X amount per month and have included recent bank statements for verification.

Make this decision easy for them. Landlords always have lots of questions, especially if you're self-employed. Giving them the answers up front with documentation to back it up will expedite the process, and get you into your new apartment sooner.

How to Pay Your Taxes

A Quick Note: All of the information below pertains to taxes in the United States. Every country works differently so do research on self-employment taxes specific to your country. Also, I am by no means a tax professional. My goal here is to help you better understand the process of paying self-employment taxes so you're ready when April 15th rolls around.

My First Job

When I was 16 years old I started my first job working at a pizza place. It paid minimum wage, but I was happy to be making any money at all. I started in the middle of a billing cycle so I didn't get my first check until three weeks after I started working. I had done several intense training days and a few 20-hour weeks, so I figured the check should be pretty decent. "I'm no *mathemagician*," I thought to myself, "but minimum wage x 75 hours or so = at least a thousand dollars." When I opened the envelope, I was shocked. Surely there was a misprint on the check.

The amount was drastically less than I expected. On closer inspection, I could see how many hours I had worked (75 or so) and how much money I had earned (a bit less than a thousand dollars), but then there was another category subtracting money: taxes.

The pizza place was automatically deducting taxes out of every paycheck. This is standard for anyone with a traditional day job. And then at the end of the year, you punch a couple numbers into TurboTax® and, if it's at all like the commercials, the computer says, "You get a $1,000 rebate," and it pretty much feels like winning the lottery.

But you don't work at a pizza place, or the GAP, or a bank. You're a professional musician. Unfortunately for us, self-employment taxes are a little more complicated. Let's break this down so you know what to do. When April 15th rolls around it's not going to feel like winning the lottery, but you're also not going to be thinking, "Where am I going to get money to pay my taxes?"

First Things First

Taxes are a pain in the ass, but they're also crucial to our society. I don't like paying taxes either, but I do like driving on paved roads, checking books out of my local library, knowing there are firefighters on duty, and all of the other nice things those taxes provide. It sucks, but it doesn't. So pay your taxes, and don't whine about it.

Also, if you're just starting your career as a professional musician you may not even make enough money to have to file taxes. Whether or not you need to pay taxes depends on your filing status, age, income, dependency status, and a few other special requirements. There are lots of websites that can help you determine your status. I'm a fan (and not a paid spokesperson) of www.efile.com.

Think About Taxes All Year

When I worked at the pizza place, they did all the tax work for me. "Doing my taxes" at the end of the year just meant double checking the math and making up the difference. When I made the jump to being a professional musician, I had to do the math myself. If you take nothing else away from this chapter, take this: *You should be thinking about your taxes all year long.*

The initial confusion and disappointment I experienced when my pizza paycheck was less than I expected was one thing, but if you don't think about your taxes all year long, multiply those feelings by 50 and add some dread; "I owe *how* much?"

Pay Quarterly

Not only should you be thinking about taxes all year long, you're required by law[18] to do so. Self-employed taxpayers are required to make estimated quarterly payments, in addition to an annual tax return (the one due April 15th).

Don't think of this as a bad thing though. Paying your taxes four times a year means less work leading up to April 15th. While you're technically required to pay quarterly taxes, many self-employed musicians still only pay yearly and it works out fine. I'm not recommending this method (based on

---

[18] Visit www.irs.gov and do a search for "self-employed individuals".

the law mentioned above) but it does happen.

Whichever route you choose, don't put it off. The longer you wait, the more you're going to hate yourself in April.

Different Tax Forms

As a self-employed professional musician, there are two main types of tax forms you'll encounter.

1099-MISC

This is the form you'll deal with most often. As a musician, you are usually hired as an "independent contractor." At the end of the year, the person who hired you includes how much they paid you in their taxes. They send that information to the government, and you'll receive a 1099 from that person or company if they paid you more than $600 in a calendar year. The more people you work with, the more 1099 forms you'll get. Last year I had about 15.

A 1099 form only reports how much money you were paid. The employer does not deduct taxes so you are responsible for doing the math and paying them yourself.

W2

This is the standard tax form for traditional employment arrangements. The employer automatically deducts taxes out of every paycheck you receive (like the pizza place did for me). You'll get a W2 form at the end of the year summarizing all the taxes taken out. Then you double-check the math to make sure the taxes taken out are all correct. This form is common for ongoing jobs, like teaching at an academy or working part time at a church.

The Bad News

We're just going to rip this off like a bandage and get it over with. The following were the federal tax rates in 2017 when I was writing this book. When you read this book in the future (or it's read to you by your cyborg assistant while cruising in your self-driving hover car) check back with the IRS for an update. I just want to give you a big picture starting point.

Income Tax (Single Filing Status)[19]

Rate	Taxable Income Bracket	Tax Owed
10%	$0 to $9,325	10% of Taxable Income
15%	$9,325 to $37,950	$932.50 plus 15% of the excess over $9,325
25%	$37,950 to $91,900	$5,226.25 plus 25% of the excess over $37,950

There are higher tax brackets than 25%, but if you're reading this book, I'm going to assume you don't fall into them.

In addition to income tax, musicians also have to pay self-employment tax. This is your share of the Social Security and Medicare taxes. Everyone else pays this too; it's just that their traditional employer deals with it as a withholding along with all of the other taxes.

---

[19] Tax Foundation. Table 1. Single Taxable Income Tax Brackets and Rates, 2017. (https://taxfoundation.org/2017-tax-brackets/)

Self-Employment Tax[20]

15.3%: 12.4% for Social Security (old-age, survivors, and disability insurance) and 2.9% for Medicare (hospital insurance)

State Tax

The two sets of numbers listed above are for federal taxes only. You will also owe state taxes, but those are typically significantly less. Since those vary from state to state, do some research to determine the specific rates in both your state and any other state in which you perform. A quick Google search with the name of the state and the word "taxes" should get you where you need to go.

What Does It All Mean?

Depending on your tax bracket, at the end of the year, you'll owe somewhere between 23.3% and 38.3% of your annual income. It stings, I know. This means one big thing for you: You should save money throughout the year so you aren't blindsided when it's time to pay up.

The amount you should save varies based on your tax bracket, but it's better to save throughout the year than panic about where you're going to get the money from when your taxes are due. When you get $100 from a gig, don't think of it as $100. Think of it as $80, or $70, or whatever you've determined the percentage to be based on your tax bracket. As soon as you deposit the money into your bank account, transfer a portion of it to a savings account specifically dedicated to your taxes.

---

[20] IRS. Self-Employment Tax Rate. (https://www.irs.gov/businesses/small-businesses-self-employed/self-employment-tax-social-security-and-medicare-taxes)

Deductions: The Silver Lining

While you're recovering from the "I have to give the government how much?" blow, let me cheer you up. When you file your taxes, you not only report your income, but also your business-related expenses. This includes anything that you've spent money on throughout the year (or quarter) that directly contributed to you being a professional musician. This includes, but is not limited to:

Music Equipment
- Musical Instruments
  Instruments can be deducted as a one-time expense or set as a "straight line depreciation" which means that the cost is evenly deducted over a period of several years. Keep your receipts.
- Musical Gear
  This includes any musical gear that isn't an instrument. Cables, straps, pedals, strings, picks, sheet music, and anything else that you can get at Guitar Center® is deductible. Keep your receipts.
- Computer
  If you bought a computer or an iPad in the last year, and you use it for your business, that's deductible. Keep your receipts.
- Recording Costs
  If you recorded an album, any musician fees, studio fees, duplication costs, or marketing costs are all tax deductible. Keep your receipts.

Administration and Promotion
- Website
  Remember how you made an awesome website to promote your startup? You get to write off the hosting cost. Keep your receipts.
- Business Cards
  The awesome business cards that you made are also deductible. Keep your receipts.

- Books

  If you bought any books about music, the music business (ahem, like this one), or business in general, you get to write them off. Scroll through your Amazon orders (receipts) and total them up!

- Office Supplies

  This includes any physical office supplies such as paper, a printer, pens, or any other items you use to do your work. Receipts necessary.

- Professional Fees

  If you hire an accountant to help with your taxes (more on that in a moment), you can write that off. This also includes fees associated with other professional services, like a lawyer. Just make sure you keep your receipts.

- Childcare

  If you're a parent, you may be eligible to for a big tax write off for your childcare. This varies by state and situation, so do some research. Oh, also, keep your receipts.

- Home Office

  If you spend part of your time working from home, you can write off a percentage of your rent and utilities. Just estimate what percent of your home is dedicated to your business. You probably don't get receipts for your rent, but you can take a picture of your rent check or note it on your bank statement.

- Phone Bill

  If you use your phone for business, you also get to write off a percentage of your bill. Estimate the percentage of business vs. personal use and deduct it! Receipts (monthly phone bill) still necessary.

Travel

- Gas Mileage

  As a musician, you drive all over the place. Keep a record of how many work-related miles you drive and add them all up at the end of the year. You'll get to

write off between 50 to 55 cents per mile driven. This also includes parking fees. Keep your parking receipts.
- Car

Because you use your car for business, you can deduct a percentage of your payments, maintenance, and repair costs. Calculate what percentage you think you drive it for business vs. personal use. Guess what? Receipts.
- Hotels

If you have an out-of-town gig and need to stay in a hotel, you can write that off too. What do you need to do this? REEECEEEEEIPTS!

Miscellaneous
- Lessons

If you took lessons from someone this past year, that falls under "continuing education" which is completely deductible. Receipt if you can.
- Student Loan Payments

If you're making monthly student loan payments, you can write those off on your taxes. Log in to your loan site and they'll give you more specific information on how much you should be writing off. It's basically like a big receipt.
- Music Purchases

While we're talking about continuing education, this also includes music purchases and concert tickets. File your iTunes receipts as soon as you get them!
- Wardrobe

If you bought clothes specifically for your job as a musician, write 'em off. This also includes dry cleaning costs. Did you keep your receipts?
- Food

You can write off food expenses as long as it was a "business meeting." This includes dinner at a gig or lunch with your band as you discuss where you want to record your next album. You know what you need though? Your receipts.

As you can see, there are a lot of things that you can write off on your taxes. And so many receipts! The deductions don't translate dollar for dollar (each category is a little different), but including all of them will considerably lower your amount owed. In case you missed it, you'll need to save receipts to prove that you actually did spend money on this stuff. Please don't store them in an old shoebox, it's almost 2020; there's an app for that.

Taxes Are Complicated

Now that you have a better understanding of what to expect and what to deduct, you are much better equipped for the upcoming tax season. Even if you have a good grasp on this stuff, taxes are still unbelievably confusing. I know how it works and the deductions that are allowed, but I'm not going to pretend to know how to calculate the exact numbers and file the paperwork. That's so incredibly complicated that there are people who make a living figuring it all out for you. Speaking of which: get a good CPA!

After you've compiled and calculated all of your income and deduction data, take that information to a certified public accountant. Google "CPA" and your city and call up several different accountants. Ask them if they have experience filing taxes for self-employed people, or even musicians. You'll get a good idea of their experience and whether or not they'll be a good fit for you from these phone calls.

I know you're probably thinking, "After all this, I still have to pay an accountant to do my taxes?" Unfortunately, yes, but let me say this: paying a CPA to handle your taxes is the best $100-$150 you'll spend all year. Plus, you'll be able to deduct the cost from next year's taxes. Keep your receipt!

Book Bonus: Free Tax Deductions Spreadsheet

You seem like a pretty cool person, so to make tax season even easier for you, I've whipped up a free Tax Deductions Spreadsheet. Visit www.startupmusician.co/bookbonus to download an Excel or Numbers file, fill in the blanks (for all the categories mentioned above), and the spreadsheet will do the math for you. Then you can send it off to your CPA (with your receipts) and they'll take care of the rest.

P.S. Save your receipt!

CHAPTER 17

COMPETITION & TROMBONE W/ ERIK HUGHES

Photo: Jeremy David

I'm a bass player and as a bass player, I have an unfair advantage; almost every single style of music needs a bass player. There's *lots* of work for bass players. But what about less common instruments, like the trombone?

Erik Hughes is proof that it's possible to make a living as a musician, even if you play trombone. He's performed and recorded with Michael Bublé, Kanye West, and Kurt Elling, and appeared on *Conan*. He keeps very busy as a performer, session player, and teacher, and since he plays trombone, I wanted to sit down with him and pick his brain.

# # #

What kinds of things make up your job?

I primarily perform playing trombone. Up until pretty recently it was 100% performance but I've had some teaching experiences come up, so it's nice to have those things also during the week. It's a lot of playing, some studio work, and now teaching.

What genre of music do you play most often?

I would say it's mostly jazz and commercial type music. On the jazz side, it's mostly in big bands. I don't do a ton of small group stuff; the trombone tends to be called more for big bands. And then I do horn section stuff, in wedding or corporate bands or with artists, and then studio work can be whatever. There's not a lot of classical music. That would be the only thing I don't do a ton of.

What kind of teaching do you do?

I teach private lessons through a few schools. I have some students at an elementary school and then a middle school and high school. I go in after school and teach private lessons. I've also been doing some work at the Los Angeles

College of Music, which is in Pasadena, and there I just teach. I do a class where I coach the horn players. It's like a full band scenario and I'm just there to help out the horn players.

What is one thing you are particularly good at?

When I first was starting to play in Los Angeles, the thing that helped me stand out was being able to improvise, which is not something that everyone who plays trombone can do. There are certain instruments like the saxophone where people are sort of expected to improvise, but trombone isn't necessarily that way. Being able to do it, I think initially helped me to stand out from the crowd. At the same time it's LA and there's tons of musicians so you really have to be able to do everything.

What does an average week of work look like for you?

I do a couple of rehearsal bands. Those are pretty constant; I do one on Monday and one on Sunday night. My teaching gigs are pretty constant too. I try to combine them into as few days as possible, sort of just stack them all together, which is not always possible. That tends to fluctuate from semester to semester depending on what the schools' schedules are for everything. So I'll probably have a couple days of teaching. Those are the constants.

The weekends are different every week. I usually have something on Fridays and Saturdays for sure, although that also fluctuates. And then there are random rehearsals for those gigs, or for other things will pop up during the week. Schedule wise it's pretty hectic; things are changing around all the time. I only have a couple things that are really consistently the same.

Do you have any sort of regular schedule or routines?

I've only been out of school for a couple of years also so

I'm still very much figuring all this stuff out. I used to try to have a very specific routine every day but I figured out really quickly that wasn't the correct thing for me. It just didn't work at all because things are always changing around like, "Oh I'm gonna work out this morning" and then the night before you end up getting a session or something that conflicts with that and then you end up never doing it and honestly, it was pretty frustrating.

So the way I do it now is to know the things I want to do within that routine and fit them in as they work out. Like right now I'm trying to exercise in the mornings at least three days a week, which doesn't always work out, but I try my best. But I don't put that on a specific day. I just say, "Okay, I'm going to try to do it three mornings," and then I figure out which three mornings I'm going to have time to do that this week and work it in that way. It's the same thing with practicing and other things. I figure out a number of times I want to do something in a week and then figure out how to fit that into everything else depending on how things fall into place. So far it's working a little bit better.

What does your actual "work" look like?

It definitely depends on the gig. Sometimes you'll have a gig and there's literally no way you can prepare for it because you don't have the music. *Maybe* you know what the music is so you can listen to it but as a horn player, a lot of times, there's not a ton of preparation, not as much as I would say a rhythm section player has to do. A lot of times we'll just have charts and as long as you're a good reader you can read the charts.

A lot of what I do is sort of extra preparation. Maybe I'll have a jazz gig and I know I have a solo on something so I'll prepare that solo to make sure that I really can do it. It's sort of of weird, but sometimes it's more preparation than is actually needed. For lessons I think about what each individual student needs that particular week. It's mostly thinking about it, I think.

And I would say that a lot of the work that I do is just making sure that my abilities are at the top of where they need to be, not for a specific gig but just in general, knowing that I'll be able to do what I need to do when I get to a specific work place type of situation.

How much work is out there for horn players? Is it similar to other instruments?

My current philosophy is that everything has its checks and balances. I think it is just as hard or easy to get work for everybody. For instance, with bass versus trombone, pretty much every band needs a bass player and they don't necessarily need a trombone player. However, there are fewer trombone players than bass players so it works out. I don't know how true that is but it seems like maybe that's one of those checks and balances.

There may be less work for trombone players but there are also fewer trombone players capable of doing that work. There probably are more gigs for bass players than there are for trombone players but I'm not sure if that makes it easier or harder to get gigs. At least that seems like how it might be. I haven't done any scientific experimentation or anything... Maybe we should!

What is kind of frustrating as a trombone player sometimes is that it's usually the last instrument to be added. It's like, "saxophone, and then maybe a trumpet and then *maybe* if we're going crazy, put the trombone player in there." Having that full three-part horn section sound is something that people appreciate but don't necessarily *know* that they appreciate. They'll just be like, "Man this sounds better for some reason," but they don't always associate that with "Oh there are *three* horn players," instead of just one playing a horn line written for three with an overdub.

Do you have any non-music hobbies?

I think video games would be a pretty major hobby of mine. I've played video games my whole life. A lot of my earlier friends were because of our video games. My girlfriend and I play video games together sometimes. I used to play with my dad all the time. It's just always been a part of my life.

What is the personal side of your life like?

I live in an apartment with my girlfriend; right now it's just us two. We've got a cat. As far as having an apartment as opposed to a house goes, for a horn player, it works out pretty well for me personally. I can see all of the cars out there so I know who's home and who's not when I want to practice. I get pretty self conscious about annoying people; but if I know that they're not home then it's cool.

Are you able to practice here?

During the day I can definitely practice without a mute or anything. If for whatever reason I want to play at like two in the morning, I have a silent brass mute. It makes the trombone essentially silent and then I can put headphones on and listen to it.

What is the hardest part about being a freelance musician?

The hardest part for me is scheduling and all aspects of that. So on a personal level, how do I hang out with my friends that don't do freelance music? Our schedules are completely opposite. I mean we're sitting here right now at 1:40 p.m. on a Tuesday. What friends can I hang out with other than those who play music, you know? Maybe unemployed ones? So that part's hard.

And then I don't have an assistant or anything so funneling the gigs and rehearsals and everything, just trying to make sure you don't double book things, being on top of all of that stuff is probably the hardest part. It's not what you think of when you're like, "I want to be a musician." There's also all of this administrative stuff that I have to do. I think that's the hardest part, for me at least.

A common misconception about being a full-time musician is that you'll be playing music all the time. The music part is the fun part. The administrative stuff, not so much. But the all of that scheduling, emailing, following up about the check that was supposed to arrive already, paying taxes, running your suit to the cleaners, that's the stuff that makes it possible for your play music for a living. It's absolutely worth it.

If you could play one show with one artist, dead or alive, who would it be and why?

I think as a horn player it would have to be Earth, Wind & Fire, back in their prime though, like 1970s Earth, Wind & Fire. I just watched those videos on YouTube and I'm pretty sure you can't have any more fun as horn player than doing one of their gigs.

Remember how Zach Rudulph wanted to be in Earth Wind and Fire? We should start a tribute band!

Even if you play a less common instrument, there's a way to make a living doing it. There may be less work, but there's also less competition, and this can work in your favor. Remember the concept of niching down? This is exactly what Erik is doing, and he's gotten to play with some pretty amazing artists in the process.

CHAPTER 18
WORK/LIFE BALANCE

The Theme of Every "Dad" Movie. Ever.

Making a career out of music is an odd thing. On the one hand, if you love playing music and you're good at it, it can be a great career choice. You've probably heard the phrase. "If you find something you love to do, you'll never work a day in your life!" This is a fun idea and it's pretty popular. You just need to find the thing you love to do and then make a living doing it. That sounds easy and amazing! You can live your dreams *and* make lots of money!

But this line of thinking suffers from the same poor logic as the ending of most "over-worked dad" movies (many of them starring Tim Allen circa 1994). Let me explain.

Divorced or widowed dad (Tim Allen) has been distant from his sweet 8-10 year old child primarily because he's "just been so busy at the office." He wears a suit with giant lapels and carries around a pager *and* a flip phone (Google it). He's too preoccupied with his work to focus on his son. As the movie progresses, they go through some crazy antics (wild summer camp, fantastical adventure, becoming Santa Clause, etc.) and it always ends like this: in the closing scene, in the one moment that summarizes the entire movie, Tim Allen has to choose whether to answer his ringing cell phone or stay for his son's baseball game. And it always ends with Tim Allen throwing his cell phone into a lake, showing (with *deep* symbolism) that he would rather spend time with his son.

That's a great ending for a movie, but there's a problem. NOW TIM ALLEN DOESN'T HAVE A JOB.

The alternative ending is that after Tim Allen throws said cell phone in the lake, he decides to open his *own* firm so he can spend *more* time with his son and less time serving the corporate suits. Because, you know, the money, planning, time, stress, and mindset needed to launch your own business works *really* well with attending weekly little league games. Oh, Tim Allen is the coach now too? Perfect.

The Balancing Act

Pursuing a realistic work/life balance is tough, but it's a very real part of being a Startup Musician.

But you're thinking, "I love music!" and I'm sure you do. It's a great career, but that whole "never working a day in your life" thing? That's nonsense.

When you make the move from amateur to pro, your relationship with music changes. It's like the transition from "just friends" to dating. You're not just hanging out with music; you're pursuing a potential future with music. You aren't just someone who loves music anymore. Now you're an entrepreneur building a business fueled by art. And I don't think it's an industry secret that business and art have always been somewhat at odds with each other.

One of the most important things you will do as professional musician is set realistic expectations for what the work actually looks like. It's so easy to romanticize our music careers that sometimes we don't see the work for what it really is.

The time you spend actually *performing* music isn't the work. That's the fun part, the icing on the cake. The hours of practicing your instrument in a room by yourself when *no one* is telling you to; *transcribing* and *listening* to new music and experimenting with new sounds, or notes, or chords; learning new songs; charting out your part; time spent getting to know other musicians; dealing with difficult people; meeting with clients; updating your website and social media; loading in and loading out; rehearsal; learning how to use Logic or Ableton or ProTools; practicing with a metronome; choosing to get better at this stuff instead of watching Netflix; THAT IS THE WORK.

Starting your own business to spend more time with your family is a great way to end a feel-good comedy, but it's not reality. Just because you work for yourself doing something you love doesn't mean that it's not work.

"Find a job you love and you'll never work a day in your life?" Not exactly. Here's how it really goes: Find a job you love and you'll love the work that you do.

This is the *only* reason you should consider a career as a professional musician. If you're getting into this to make a lot of money, there are literally hundreds of other professions that pay much more money for much less time. But if, like me, you can't imagine doing anything else (or you're *really* like me and just aren't good at much else) then a career in music might be for you.

Sometimes the song you have to play is terrible. Sometimes your private student acts like a turd. Sometimes it's incredibly frustrating. Taxes are a pain. You don't make as much money as your friends. You drive a run down station wagon.

The only way *anyone* in their right mind would sign up for this is if they're getting something more than money out of it. And that's the love of music. When I'm on stage and the groove feels just right, or when a student makes a breakthrough, or when I hear the final mix, all is right in the world. The "shortcomings" of a career in music don't matter because I get to *make music* for a living.

Being Your Own Boss

In the past 10 years, there's been a big shift in workplace mentality. Maybe it's a generational thing. People are starting to look beyond 9-to-5 desk jobs with benefits. They aren't looking to put in 30 years at one company and retire at 65. More and more people are striking out on their own, kick starting their own projects, earning their living independently (movie Tim Allen would be so proud). There are no guarantees and it's not as secure, but these visionaries just aren't that concerned with being part of an established company. They just want enough to provide a comfortable living doing something they love.

Being self-employed can be a great thing. I'm definitely a fan. But it's not all unicorns and rainbows. I have friends who work traditional jobs who often say things like, "Wow, that's really cool! I wish I could do that! It must be amazing to have all that freedom, to be your own boss!"

Working for yourself has definite perks, but it also has its drawbacks because the buck stops with you. You are the CEO, the CFO, the IT department, HR, and marketing.

The CEO – That's You!

If you're going to be your own boss, you have to be the boss. I don't mean you have to be a boss in the baller sense of the word. I mean you have to set the vision and goals *and* get the work done. You are the chief executive officer *and* the employee. If you applied for an entry level job flipping burgers at McDonald's, do you think after the interview they would say, "Hey, actually, we've been looking for a new manager too. Do you want that job? You'll be the boss. You'll still flip burgers, but I also need you to run the place. Oh, and we don't have any other employees."

That doesn't sound like something you would sign up for, but that's what you're doing when you become a Startup Musician. *You are your own boss.* With great power comes greater responsibility. If you're a terrible boss and let your employee (you) sleep all day, show up late to things, and don't keep track of the company finances, your startup is doomed.

The CFO – Also You

You're not just in charge of mission, vision, goals, and objectives; you're also in charge of the finances. You are the chief financial officer. Living on flexible income takes some getting used to. As a freelance musician, you don't get a check on the 15th and 30th every month. You get like 17 checks on the 1st, 3rd, 4th, 7th, 9th, 11th, 12th, 14th, 16th, 18th, 20th, 21st, 24th, 25th, 26th, 29th, and 30th of the month. And then the next month you only get four checks. It's a lot to juggle. Once you get used to it, it's not so bad, but if you're used to a twice a month check, you're in for a fun change. And don't forget about paying your taxes. Seriously. Don't forget to save for that.

The IT Department – You Can Do That, Right?

Setting up the website. That's your job. Keeping it

current, that's the job for the Marketing Department (spoiler alert – also you). If your gear needs tweaking or repair, you do it, or find and pay the person who can. Software. You're going to need to stay on top of the tools that best serve your startup. There is always something to learn or practice.

HR – You Too

"Making your own hours" doesn't mean that you get to wake up at noon, stay in your pajamas all day, and eat Totino's Pizza Rolls® for every meal. You're confusing that with being in junior high.

Making your own hours means that it's your decision when to start working, and equally important, when to stop working. Since you are your own boss, you're in charge. Do you feel good about the one hour you spent working on music today compared to the five you spent doing other stuff? For some people it's hard to get motivated to start.

For others, the challenge is knowing when to stop. Because there's no one to *tell* you when to stop, it can be difficult to do so. You always feel like there's more you could be doing. You *could* be even *more* successful. You *could* be even *better* at your thing. You need to get a feel for when it's time to take a break, and live the other parts of your life. Go hang out with your friends, watch Netflix, eat something, and get some sleep.

Marketing – Totally you

Is your website current? Drop a line on the social media platform de jour. Connect with another musician and plan a coffee run. Keeping your startup fresh in people's minds is also part of running the business. Zach Rudulph outsourced this task when his budget permitted and you'll get there someday. Until then, you run the marketing and PR department too.

There are a lot of moving pieces when you run a startup! The good news is that while you are ultimately responsible for ALL OF THE THINGS, it's possible to do this without losing your mind. Here's how I do it.

Separate "Boss You" from the Rest of You

You are more than your work. You are more to you than just "Tevin the Drummer" or "Chaz the Singer." It's important to separate your *self* from your *work*. This will help you stay sane. If your identity is completely tied up in your career as a musician, you're in for a bumpy ride. Your emotions will fluctuate as dramatically as your bank account. If your identity is solely based on your success as a professional musician, than you'll take *every* failure personally.

This is why it helps think of being a professional musician as a startup. If there's only one "you" (you as a person + you as a professional musician), then everything is on your shoulders and you end up taking everything personally.

If, however, you shift your mentality to that of running a startup, then it's not just you. There's a boss, remember? Yes, technically, the boss is still you, but I want you to think of your startup as two very different sides of "you."

Here's the hierarchy: You>Boss You>Employee You.

Pictured Left to Right: Me, Boss Me, and "My Nephew Who Is A Sweet Kid But Just Needs a Little Motivation" Me (also known as "Employee" Me).

There's "Boss" you and "Employee" you. Boss you is in charge of the big picture stuff, all of that stuff from earlier in the chapter about setting goals, making schedules, setting a routine, and choosing new things to focus on and learn. Employee you is the person who has to execute the plan.

Boss you is the one who says, "yes" to the call, takes your suit to the dry cleaners, maps out your week and says "I have rehearsal on Thursday, so I need to learn the songs on Wednesday." Boss you is also in charge of growing the company, adding new services, and coming up with new ideas. Employee you is the one who learns the songs, goes to rehearsal, wears the suit, and plays the gig.

This dual boss/employee mentality can help you better approach some of the challenges of being a Startup Musician.

- Maybe you're an introvert who *hates* talking to people. Boss you knows that you need to get better at talking to people to naturally network and expand the brand. Boss you creates some opportunities to do that. Employee you digs in and does what the boss wants, because you're not being you, you're Employee you.

- If Employee you really wants to hang with your friends at Disneyland for the third time this week, Boss you needs to step in to remind you of your long-term financial goals and suggest that you pass this time around.

When you are able to separate your identity as a professional musician from your identity as a human being, you give yourself a sanity buffer. If a project fails, or you play horribly, or you're fired from a gig, that's Employee you, and Boss you takes care of Employee you. You figure out what happened, and correct, retrain, and support yourself to get back on track.

In traditional jobs, when a boss has serious issues with the employee, he or she will take it to the manager. In our world, Manager you is the real you (as in you as a person), and you can decide what to do from there. This is for the extreme cases, like maybe being a professional musician isn't for you after all. If it comes to that, that's okay, but don't have a mini life crisis after every gig! Let Boss you handle that.

Speaking as someone who has started many things and then failed at most of them, I'll tell you: having this separation between you and your work is incredibly beneficial.

The Self Doubt Pep Talk

Attention Boss you: Keep this one in your back pocket for the days when self-doubt comes crashing down and Employee you needs some encouragement.

When you're self-employed, your income and workload vary from month to month. As you've heard from multiple musicians in this book, this can fill you with *all kinds* of self-doubt.

> "I had more gigs last month, and this month I don't know how I'm going to pay rent. I'm worthless as a musician. No one likes me. I wonder if Terry is still managing my old department at Best Buy? Maybe I should give him a call."

If I had a dollar for every time I've thought this about myself, I'd actually have a lot of money (which, come to think of it, would actually solve my dilemma). This is an incredibly common thing among freelance musicians, but no one really talks about it.

There's a strong assumption in Western culture that you should graduate high school, go to college, find a job, and climb the ladder of success for the rest of your life. It's ingrained deep down. It's in our movies, television, language, and the way we've set up our society. This is what your grandparents did and likely what your parents did as well. There's absolutely nothing wrong with this life model, it's just that it doesn't fit particularly well with being a freelance musician. When you get a gig, even if it's regular work, it isn't going to last forever. The tour is going to end, the album is going to wrap, the bar is going to close, or the artist is going to "go in a different direction."

In conversations with other musicians for the Startup Musician podcast, this book, and just in general, I've noticed that no one ever fully feels like they've "made it." There's no freeze frame while the credits roll. They quite never feel like they've arrived at the thing they're going to be doing forever; it could all end tomorrow. And these are musicians doing awesome things all over the world! These are the musicians you want to be, that you assume have it all together. I can't tell you how encouraging this if for me to hear this because I feel THE EXACT SAME WAY.

The traditional life plan is like driving into a cul-de-sac. It's definitely comfortable and you can see everything from where you stand, but there's nothing quite like the open road. My career has had its share of twists and turns. I've had the opportunity to do some really cool stuff and I support my family as a freelance musician. It's incredible! But at the same time, I frequently ask myself, "Is this it? Is this my peak?"

That said, there's one question I've learned to completely disregard which is: "Is this what I'm going to be doing for the rest of my life?" No need to ask because the answer will always be a resounding "NO!"

There is no job security in this profession. That's simultaneously frightening and beautiful. Frightening because I never know what I'm going to be doing beyond two months from today (THIS COULD BE THE END!). Beautiful because I get to do so many different things. I play lots of different types of music, with lots of different people, in lots of different places. How awesome is that?

So, if you're feeling stuck, or feel like you're not doing the things you really want to be doing with your music career, don't worry. Wherever you're at right now is not where you'll be in a year. Embrace the frightening beauty of that fact, and just keep going.

When you come back to this page in five years you'll thank me.

The Five-Year Update

WARNING: DO NOT READ THIS UNTIL 5 YEARS FROM THE PURCHASE DATE OF THIS BOOK!

Oh, hey! What's up? Nice self-lacing Nikes! I love those. How you doing? You doing okay? You look a little tired. Are you burnt out? Have you played [insert current hit song here] a bajillion times? Do you feel like you're losing it a little bit? Well I have a bit of advice for you.

Call up a friend. Grab some coffee. Play a free gig. I'm not talking about doing a free gig just to not get paid. I'm talking about a gig with people you enjoy, playing music that you love. These types of gigs remind you why you got into music in the first place. They help keep you sane. If you can't find a gig with good people and good music, *go out and make one.* In place of money, you get something better: inspiration. Then you can jump back into your regular music work with a fresh mind and renewed excitement.

Well that's it for now. I hope the future is treating you well. Enjoy the flying cars!

CHAPTER 19
ENGINEERING & IDENTITY W/ MANDY ADAMS

Photo: Juliann Cheryl

Like most startup musicians, Mandy Adams has a hybrid career. She's a bass player and primarily performs and does some recording work, but she's also the project manager and an engineer working with Dale Becker at Becker Mastering in

Pasadena, CA. It's a job that looks remarkably traditional by startup standards but is still firmly under the music umbrella.

Becker Mastering has mastered albums for Neil Diamond, Tyrone Wells, and the movie *Insurgent.* Mandy does some assistant engineering with Dale, her name is on the credits for Macklemore and Ryan Lewis' album *This Unruly Mess I've Made,* but she also handles most of the administrative stuff that goes into running a small business.

We met up in the mastering studio to talk about her life, her work, and the value that we tend to ascribe to our careers.

♯ ♯ ♯

What is one thing that you are particularly good at?

I have a pretty good understanding of what goes into mastering, which really shows up in my playing, my musicianship, and what I'm doing. There's sort of an overall picture you get in the mastering process. I get to sit here for eight hours a day and listen to all kinds of music, all sorts of styles, and honestly I think that has affected my playing a lot. I get to sonically understand what's going on in a mix, and that translates into my live stuff. It's understanding, "Alright, if I play all these notes and I play them up high its gonna sound like this," and I don't want it to sound like that. That's not necessarily a "mastering engineering" thing, I just get to listen to a lot of stuff and it's not always good stuff. Sometimes it's taking the bad and saying, "definitely don't want to be doing that."

What does an average week of work look like for you?

Most of the time I'm here during the day, sort of "normal" work hours, like 10 a.m. to 6 or 7 p.m., although that's pretty flexible even if I'm not playing somewhere. A lot of times I need to be here when Dale's not here so that I can run stuff, or use the room. Sometimes that looks like having a couple mornings off but working late nights.

I guess this week would be a pretty good example. I had a rehearsal last night. I'm working on producing an EP right now so tonight and tomorrow night will probably be a lot of working on that. We had a drum session last week, so I've been getting that all together and ready for the next session. On Thursday I'll be playing with a couple of artists at an artist showcase here in town and then Friday I'm playing at a women's event. That's a church thing Friday night. And then Saturday I've got a Top 40 gig at a college. So a lot of variety keeps things interesting and fun.

What does your actual "work" look like?

At the mastering studio I do a lot of the stuff of running a small business; a lot of website upkeep and social media stuff, we're working on being better at that. I do a lot of rate negotiations with clients and explaining what's going on. Not a lot of people, not even musicians and artists, quite understand mastering. There is a lot of teaching people what's really happening here.

We work on a lot of projects at one time. We probably average 450 to 500 projects a year. Because mastering's a much quicker process than mixing or recording, our network's really wide. We're dealing with a lot of people so there's a lot of scheduling and organization that needs to happen behind the scenes. So I do a lot of that to keep Dale mastering more and scheduling less. I also do assistant work for him too, which is great, making tweaks on projects or printing different versions for people.

With my own playing, it's obviously a lot of learning songs. I'll play some synth bass and sometimes it's working out what those sounds are, or where they even go. Since I'm in the studio so much I don't get a ton of practice time to myself, not nearly as much as I'd like, so I really try to use those times that I'm prepping for a gig. I try to be really intentional to make them useful to me as a player too, trying not to just learn songs as quickly as I can but asking, "Alright, what's going on in this song? What licks are they playing that I can take to the next thing?" I have to be kind of focused in that way to get in as much in as I can, sometimes in as little time as possible.

And then there's the silly things like, I'm going straight from the studio to a gig so I'm thinking, "What am I wearing and what things will I need?" There's a mental checklist of the gear I need to have in my car when I leave at nine in the morning for my gig that's at nine at night.

What are you reading these days?

Mandy is an avid reader, particularly non-fiction. (Hey, like you're doing right now! So meta.)

Right now I'm finally reading The War of Art. I feel like I probably should have read it 10 years ago. My reading is very widespread. The War of Art is probably the closest thing to music I'll get. I'm not super into the music biographies.

Hold up. I'm so glad Mandy mentioned that book! Steven Pressfield's The War of Art is one of my favorite books. Is it weird to recommend another book in the middle of my book? Well, I'm going to. You should buy it right now. Finish this book and then go buy it.

What is the rest of your life like?

I would say that my "normal" life is sometimes hard to distinguish from my "music" life. I'm single, no kids, and a lot of my friends are musicians. Not all of them, thankfully. I do try to make relationships and social things a priority. I think it's really easy as musicians to get so into wanting to be the best and working all the time, it's just engrained in us, that there's no such thing as free time. There's just practice, or songwriting, or whatever you're *supposed* to be doing.

There can be a lot of guilt that surrounds not doing those things. I've had to work hard to be okay with grabbing coffee with friends and those things have become as important as my career. I would feel like I have a really boring, lame life if I didn't have people beside me. A lot of times those people are musicians too. Those coffee dates or going to Disneyland for the day or whatever it is, you can be multitasking I guess and that's okay, but you have to place a priority on people and not getting too inside of your own thing. It's not just, "What do I need to be doing?" but also, "Who are the people that I'm with and what am I being to the world?" There has to be more to your life than just playing bass for weddings.

Mandy has reached that sweet spot of understanding that she is more than her startup. If your entire identity is wrapped up in your career as a musician, when things don't go your way, you end up taking it personally. Mandy's emphasis on being more than her startup isn't just healthy; it's vital to her long-term success.

What is the hardest part about being a freelance musician?

Without getting too deep, I think that we as musicians, maybe just as Americans, we place a lot of value on our businesses and on how full our schedule is. When you meet another musician and tell them that you've been busy, they congratulate you like, "Good! So glad you're busy!" It means you're making money, and that's cool, but it's sort of easy to tie all of your worth and value into that.

This month *is* busy and I have a lot going on. I feel great about myself. I'm like, "Alright, people are calling me to play for them. Sweet!" Last month was not so busy. Thankfully I have my studio job that I can go to but I know a lot of people don't have that. In those famine times it's easy to sort of just circle down like, "What am I doing with my life?" when honestly those famine times don't always have to do with your skills or if you've networked enough. Sometimes the gigs just aren't there, and that's okay. You have to learn how to sort of love those down times and make use of them instead of crying yourself to sleep and wishing that somebody would call you.

She nailed it. If you have a night off, or a week off, or a month off (like pretty much every January), that doesn't mean you're worthless or that your career is over. The ebb and flow of work is part of life for a professional musician, and as frustrating as it can be, you have to remember that it's not you; it's just how the job goes.

If you could play one show with one artist, dead or alive, who would it be?

That's hard because I like variety! Right now I'm really into this band Gungor. I feel like they have a lot of variety in their music. They're kind of a musician's band so it's fun stuff, but also very relatable and they've got some hooks in there that can be "poppy". So I feel like that's the best of all worlds. If you ask me next week I might have a different answer.

Mandy's startup involves more structure than most and her gig works keeps her busy, but she's smart enough to know that even when she's not busy, it's not a sign; it's just a season. I can't over emphasize how important this mindset is to the life of a Startup Musician, but I'm sure going to try.

CHAPTER 20
THE
THRESHOLD

We're almost done here, just a few chapters left, so this is probably a good time to remind you that the basic requirement for becoming a Startup Musician, the crucial first step and most important thing is that you have to be good at something. Good enough that people will pay you to do it.

This book can't tell you how to do that. It's an entirely different conversation. But it should go without saying that in order to build a career as a professional musician, you have to be really great at something. Notice that I said *something*, not *everything*. While your startup may need multiple things in order to stay afloat, you shouldn't try to do everything. You want to be great at a few things, not mediocre at a lot of things.

Over the years I've found that there's this invisible but very real threshold for professional musicians. Those above the threshold are "good enough" to make a living as a professional musician. Those below it aren't.

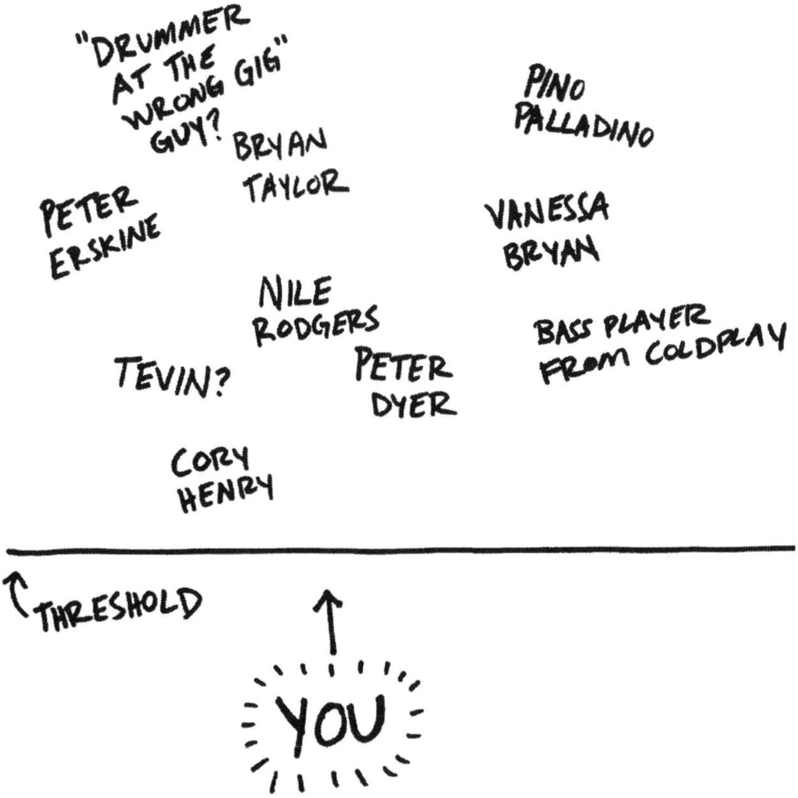

"DRUMMER AT THE WRONG GIG" GUY?

PINO PALLADINO

BRYAN TAYLOR

PETER ERSKINE

VANESSA BRYAN

NILE RODGERS

TEVIN?

PETER DYER

BASS PLAYER FROM COLDPLAY

CORY HENRY

THRESHOLD

YOU

The threshold is kind of an intangible thing. I'm not sure how to describe it to you, other than to say that those above the threshold "get it". They understand what being a professional musician is really like, and what it takes to succeed.

They understand musical things like how to play comfortably in all 12 keys, how to stay in time, how to make the music *feel* good, and they have ears sharp enough to know where a song is headed without verbal instruction. But they also understand the non-musical things that are part of the job like staying up late to learn songs, bringing *all* the gear you need to a gig, and showing up appropriately dressed, all while being prepared for and flexible enough to accommodate just about anything.

The goal is to get above that threshold. And it doesn't really matter how you get there. Some people go to school, get a degree, get another degree, and still never cross the threshold. Other people teach themselves by watching "Snarky Puppy Drum Covers" on YouTube, play a few gigs, and make it across.

There are a million things to learn in college, but how to be a freelance musician isn't one of them. In the end, *your degree doesn't matter*. Don't get me wrong, professional training is incredibly valuable and degrees are great for things like teaching, but in the history of modern music no one has every called someone up for any type of gig and first asked, "Where did you go to school? Do you have a degree?"

What matters *more* is getting above the threshold. You don't have to be the best, just *good enough*. Once you've crossed over, you're good enough to make it.

Are You Better than the Bass Player from Coldplay?

Every Thanksgiving (feel free to insert your own holiday here) I get together with my extended family, and since I don't have a "real" job, I get a lot of awkward questions, not least of which is, "Are you as good as _____?"

> "Hey Brandon, are you as good at bass as the bass player from Coldplay?" (I still don't know how to even begin to answer this question.)
>
> "Check out this Victor Wooten video, are you that good?" (I mean, I guess not?)
>
> "Who's better, you or the bass player singer guy from American Idol?" (Ooh, this one I can answer! Definitively me.)

It's the worst. Not only are the questions unanswerable, the entire premise behind them is wrong. Ranking musicians from 1-100 might work for an Internet listicle, but it's a horrible way to structure your startup.

Remember earlier when you chose your MVPs? Make those things your things. For Peter Dyer, it's being _the_ vintage keyboard guy. For Vanessa Bryan, it's being a great singer who is easy to work with and brings passion to every performance. For Bryan Taylor, it's the crazy sounds he makes with his drums, sticks, hands, and fingers.

Once you're above the professional musician threshold, it's not a _linear_ ranking of ability. It's a three-dimensional world of opportunities. Peter Dyer's territory is vintage synths. Zach Marsh's territory _is_ piano and composition. Who's a _better_ keyboard player? That question is irrelevant.

A better question to ask is, "Who is right for this gig?" Since they're *both* above the threshold they could both do it, but they have strengths. You're going to get a different end result depending on whom you choose, and *that's a good thing.*

Several factors play into this decision: What is this person's territory? What will they bring to the project? Are they any good? What are they like as a person? Are they easy to work with? Do they "get it"? Are they a real Tevin? All of these questions subconsciously run through the mind of anyone hiring a musician.

You are going to better than some people at some things, and not as great as others at other things. But in the end, that won't matter. The professional music world isn't a cutthroat ranking of best to worst. It isn't a competition. Work to get above the threshold, find your niche, and start building. Figure out what you're uniquely good at and focus on becoming truly great.

So *am* I better than the bass player from Coldplay? That's the wrong question. Here are some better ones:

Could I handle playing bass in Coldplay?
Would Coldplay *want* me to join the band?
Would *I* want to play bass in Coldplay?
What kinds of things am I good at?
On the Venn diagram of my startup, where do
    things overlap?
How can I best use the things I'm good at?

While Aunt Linda is *never* going to ask these questions, these are the ones you should be asking as you work to get above the threshold, wade through the opportunities, and claim your territory (right next to the bass player from Coldplay).

CHAPTER 21
THE ART OF THE PIVOT (&COFFEE) W/TROY WELSTAD

I live in the Los Angeles area and most of my work happens here. LA is one of three major music cities in the United States along with Nashville and New York. There are certainly other cities in which you can work as a professional musician, but these three tend to have the highest concentration of available work. So I was particularly excited to talk to Troy Welstad, a keyboard player who left LA for greener pastures (literally).

Troy made a name for himself in LA as a touring keyboard player working with major artists like Hilary Duff and P!nk. But a few years ago he and his wife decided to leave beautiful, smoggy, odd LA for Portland, Oregon (which is even *more* beautiful, *less* smoggy, and *much more* odd).

When I meet with Troy we kick off the interview with a tour of his setup. There's a room dominated by a large soundboard, computers, audio hardware, and a vocal isolation booth, and then, there's the basement.

Troy takes me downstairs, giddy with excitement. He's thrilled to show what he's built to someone who will truly appreciate it. It's basically the room that dreams are made of. Troy has converted the entire basement into a studio space complete with amps, drum sets, boxes of cables, microphones, stands, you name it. Troy points toward the ceiling and says, "Right here, this is where I run the cables up to connect to the control room."

Troy's home studio setup is impressive, but I'm even more struck by just how excited he is about it. Think "kid on Christmas morning excited," except that instead of toys it's expensive audio equipment, it's mid-January, and we're all grown up now.

Troy and I make our way back up to the control room where we discuss his transition out of LA, his personal life, and coffee (it *is* Portland after all).

# # #

What kinds of things make up your job?

At this point my job is basically half studio sessions and recording and half playing local gigs around Portland. I'm trying to get everything to be in the studio world but it's still a combination of things.

How long have you been in Portland?

I've been here four and a half years, five years? We moved in the summer of 2011, I think. So, coming up on five years.

How long had you been in LA?

If you count college, about 10 years, but from 2005 to 2011 most of what I was doing was touring and I didn't really have hardly any gear or a studio or anything like that.

Who are some of the artists that you toured with?

My first tour was with Ryan Cabrera. It was in the summer of 2006 and it was my first real touring gig; it was on a bus. We played the House of Blues and those kinds of mid-sized clubs all over the U.S. I was young and I hadn't done any of that stuff yet. It was just so fun, you feel like, "I did it!" the thing that we all dream about. That gig was about a year between rehearsals, promo stuff, and more rehearsal stuff for the big tour. We had a break and then we did like a winter run.

Then I think a few months later I went out for a Barry Squire audition and I got the Hilary Duff tour. That was crazy because there were 300 people lined up at center staging and then I got the call back. Wait, no, I was pouting about not getting the call back and then my buddy calls me like, "Hey Barry couldn't find your number but you got the call back so come tomorrow." They kept trying different combinations of people in the rehearsal room and they kept sending people home until it was just seven or eight of us, and they were like, "You guys got the gig."

Barry Squire is the king of the pop music cattle call audition. Almost everyone has his contact info, but that doesn't matter all that much. I know people who have called him every day for a month, trying to get an audition. When they did finally reach him, they were invited to an audition with a hundred or more other musicians.

The music director for Hilary was a guy who had also worked with P!nk, so basically that relationship led me to touring with P!nk in 2008. Then at that point I started thinking that I was really more of a creative person. I wanted to *create* music and *write* music and not just be on the road all the time, so I started to buy some gear. But then after that I still toured with A Fine Frenzy and then with Brooke Fraser.

Why Portland?

I think I just came to realize the creative part of me needed it. I wanted to be in a place where I could create, where people didn't know who I was, where I could be off the grid or live somewhere cheaper. I basically wanted to get away from *just* touring and into a role where I was able to write and produce and create, and I felt like that was recording and doing records.

I had this idealized version of Portland in my head of like, "We can just come here and drink coffee and beer and make records," and that was mostly true, but Portland's changed so much within the past five years. The costs are getting closer to California and the whole scene is changing.

What is one thing you are particularly good at?

I think one of the things that I didn't intend to do, but is part of what I do now, is sound design. I mean, I'm a

201

keyboard player first; I came up playing piano and I got super into piano in high school. When I went to college I did the "woodshed" thing; I think I had one summer where I was like, "I'm gonna play eight hours a day." I tried to do that most of the summer and I don't know how many days I actually got to eight hours, but I had that drive to be like, "I'm just gonna get insane with this." Everything has kind of come from that.

And then with some of the session stuff now, I think sonics have become more important in this musical era. So that's something that I've gotten good at. This guy just sent me a record from Nashville that he's working on. They already did keys, they just want me to do sounds and soundscapes and sweetening and ear candy. So that's something that has grown a lot.

What does an average week of work look like for you?

I get up really tired on Monday from getting up early for a church gig on Sunday. And then I'm usually catching up on some emails or doing a track that I have to get done for someone. A typical week *should* be that I'm doing send-away tracks, or maybe a producer comes over and I do a session with somebody.

This last week is probably a good sample. I had a producer come over Monday and Wednesday. I think I caught up on stuff on Tuesday. I had a writing session last night and then playing gigs on the weekends. I need to get better at taking a day off. I pretty much play and then I'm in here either doing sessions or doing a record that I'm producing or working for other producers. So that's basically the combo.

What does your actual "work" look like?

Well, a lot of the session stuff looks like me just sitting in a chair right here in front of ProTools. But if I'm producing or if I'm writing, a lot of that looks like I'm sitting at the computer building a track or working on some sort of part over here. Sometimes it can be recording with some of these beautiful keyboards. If I'm recording I usually have somebody else here to help me engineer.

There's a great young engineer in town named Ryan Short and he comes and helps me record. A lot of the stuff I'm producing for recording, drums or that kind of stuff, I pretty much don't do it without having him here. And then gigs are pretty typical; learn the tunes, get the sounds right, load up your gear, go play the gig.

Do you have any sort of regular schedule or routines?

I think the only real routine that I have is that I get up at nine or 10. A lot of days it's before that, but most workdays don't start before 10, ever. I usually go hang out at Heart Coffee for a little bit depending on what I'm working on. Last week we had this session and me and Ryan and a client, we hung out at Heart for like an hour. We had three coffees each and were having such a great time. That feeling that you have in LA, like the clock's always ticking, it doesn't feel like it's the same vibe here. I don't think it's laziness, I think it's just a different attitude, a different outlook, like, "Yeah, we're gonna get the work done but we're also gonna just hang out and enjoy life and get coffee."

So I usually get up, go find myself some coffee, and then I typically work 'til eight. Sometimes Trish and I will go out or stay in and have friends over. Sometimes the day is more doing emails or running some errands and then your session starts later in the afternoon and you work 'til midnight, that's pretty typical too.

What is your personal life like?

Trish and I have been married for coming up on nine years, which is crazy. We've been together forever, like 15 years. We were just babies when we got together. We have a baby on the way so real soon that's going to happen, and I have a little dog. We rent this house here in Southeast Portland and my family is an hour south down in Salem, Oregon. It is nice to be in the Northwest a little bit closer to family too. I think with having a kid it's going to be nicer even still to be closer to family.

What is the hardest part about being a freelance musician?

I should say that it's the rollercoaster of finances, but I actually don't think that's the hardest part. I think the hardest part is the struggle to continue to achieve what you really want to go for.

I feel that as I grow, the bar keeps going up, so I always feel like, "Man I want to get on this level now, and then I want to get to this level." I see a lot of people my age who haven't figured out their thing yet or they're struggling to get to the next level. So I don't know, I think maybe that's the hardest part; the constant feeling that you're not there yet.

It's crazy to hear someone as successful as Troy say he feels like he hasn't "made it" yet, but that's the reality of life as a startup musician. You work hard, you cross the threshold, you continue to get incrementally better, you get better paying work, higher status work, and you just keep going. While it's strange to hear Troy say it, it's also incredibly comforting, because I feel the exact same way. It's simultaneously encouraging and disappointing knowing that this feeling may never go away.

If you could play one show with one artist, dead or alive, who would it be?

I'm going to go with something that I would just have a really fun time playing. I think if I could I would play B3 in a band for someone like Sheryl Crowe. Something with amazing songs and super fun parts to play where you can have some real gear on stage. That's my answer, because otherwise it's just way too hard to decide something like that!

Troy is a great example of how a Startup Musician can cross the threshold and continue to evolve. While he used to live life as an LA-based touring keyboard player, he's now making records out of his home in Portland. Just because you don't live in LA doesn't mean you can't make a living as a professional musician. And just because you've chosen you few things to focus on doesn't mean you can't change your mind down the road.

CHAPTER 22
WHERE YOUR STARTUP ENDS UP

I'm A Startup Musician. Now What?

The world of tech startups is an exciting one, but the beginning of a startup is the most exciting part. It's all plans and ambition, designing logos, dreaming of how this app could change the world, and feeling like a million bucks when an investor shells out the first round of funding.

Then things get real.

Startups work like crazy to make their thing. The app launches. People download it. People complain about the bugs. Servers crash. Bugs get fixed. More and more people download the app. A new version comes out with additional features. People complain about how they miss the old version. This cycle goes on and on until it reaches an inevitable turning point. Regardless of the product, every startup ultimately faces three questions:

> How do we make money?
> What is this all leading to?
> Where do we go from here?

As a Startup Musician, you'll face the same questions. When you're 21, sharing an apartment with four other people, and eating Top Ramen® five times a week, nothing can get you down. You're practicing hard, dreaming of the venues you'll play, the artists you'll work with, and how much money you'll make. You put in years of hard work doing what you love and then you turn 30 and face the same questions:

> How do I make more money?
> What is this all leading to?
> Where do I go from here?

I've spent a lot of time talking to other musicians about this lately. I turned 30 in the recent past and that number seems to be a turning point in our field. You wake up one day and think, "I've done this for 10 years, where do I go from here?"

There are a few ways that tech startups answer this question, and these responses are key to understanding how you'll answer your own questions when the time comes.

Sell the Startup to a Larger Company

This is one endgame that a lot of tech startups aim for. Instagram sold to Facebook in 2012 for $1 billion[21]. Prior to that acquisition, Instagram wasn't making money. It was a very popular app, but just not profitable. But that's not

---

[21] "Facebook buys Instagram for $1 billion, turns budding rival into its standalone photo app" TechCrunch. (April 9, 2012).

Instagram's problem anymore, now it's Facebook's problem. In 2013 Yahoo bought Tumblr for $1.1 billion[22]. Tumblr's profitability is now Yahoo's task. In 2010 Apple paid about $200 million to purchase a small startup called Siri[23]. Siri itself doesn't have to be profitable anymore. Apple has $246 billion in cash[24], so they'll figure it out (Please, tell me they'll figure Siri out!).

When a tech startup becomes part of a larger, already profitable, company the financial pressure eases up. Even if Instagram loses money over a month, Facebook as a whole is doing just fine, so it evens out. Instagram can keep doing its thing without having to worry about how it's going to keep the lights on.

In the world of *Startup Musicians,* this looks like merging with someone who has a more traditional job. The financial support of a spouse or partner with a regular income can help smooth out the sporadic cash flow of the freelance life.

You know that musician who has INSANE gear, the newest everything, and hardly works, and it doesn't seem to add up, until you meet their spouse, Professor Dr. Moneybags, Ph.D. Esquire? Yeah, that's not me. I married a Startup Musician (and she's amazing).

Hubie Wang's wife has a traditional job and they work to balance their income, schedules, and lives around each other. It's going well. But Vanessa Bryan had a very different experience. If you're going to merge your startup with another party, make sure that both of you have a clear

---

[22] Nicholas Carlson. "Marissa Mayer: Here's why I just bought Tumblr for $1.1 billion" Business Insider. (May 20, 2013).

[23] Erick Schonfeld. "Silicon Valley buzz: Apply paid more than $200 million for Siri to get into mobile search" TechCrunch. (April 28, 2010).

[24] Paul R. La Monica. "Apple has $246 billion in cash, nearly all overseas" CNN Money. (February 1, 2017).

understanding of what startup life is really like.

Fizzle Out and Close Up Shop

Do you remember Yik Yak? It was an anonymous social media app that launched in 2013. It was a good idea, but was plagued with several college harassment scandals. After consistently losing users, and with no path to real profitability, Yik Yak shut down in 2017[25]. The app itself worked fine and was popular among its users for a time. The company even managed to raise $73 million in funding and reached a peak valuation of $400 million. But because of its anonymous harassment problems no larger company wanted to buy it. So the developers closed up shop. Days before Yik Yak shut down, payment company Square hired its engineering team.

For every Instagram success story there are at least a *thousand* Yik Yak stories. Not every tech startup has what it takes to be successful. A lot of factors play into a company's success or failure, but ultimately the market decides which ones stick around.

Some Startup Musicians fizzle out too. For every Mandy Adams or Erik Hughes, there are at least a thousand musicians who go to music school and try to make a living, but ultimately decided to close up shop and change careers. Maybe they want to make more money, have a more traditional schedule, or spend more time with their family. Maybe they just aren't getting much work as a musician. Whatever the reason, there are *a lot* of professional musicians who don't make it past age 25, 28, or *especially* 30.

The life of a Startup Musician isn't for everyone, and that's okay. I bet the Yik Yak team doesn't regret building their app, even though they ultimately ended it. My friends

---

[25] Nick Statt. "Yik Yak, once valued at $400 million, shuts down and sells of engineers for $1 million" The Verge. (April 28, 2017).

who tried their hand at being a professional freelance musician and then decided to do something else don't regret their musical efforts; they just decided it was time to move on to another career option.

While it may seem a little sad at first, closing up shop is a valid option for your startup. Work for as long as you can, enjoy the ride, and eventually settle into a different career.

Keep Going and Stay Afloat

There are hundreds (maybe thousands) of "To Do" apps out there. They let you set reminders, organize folders, list out subtasks, and even share tasks with other people. But let's face it, they're all pretty much the same. They're all...fine.

And then there's Clear.

Clear launched in 2012 to great fanfare. People loved the simplicity of this app. Clear offered no subtasks, no reminders, and no group sharing. Just a list of things you had to do, laid out in a simple way. It's difficult for me to describe just how different Clear is, other than to say that it's wonderfully, beautifully simple. That's why it's been on my phone home screen since it launched.

Clear is made by a company called Realmac Software. It's not a huge company and it isn't owned by a larger company. It was founded in 2002 and has never gone public. While Realmac Software is surely profitable, it isn't playing in the hundreds of millions or billions league like some of the other tech companies mentioned in this book.

Realmac just keeps pressing on. The team knows they're not going to be working on the same scale as Facebook or Dropbox, but that doesn't bother them. They are focused on one thing: making great products that their customers enjoy. They've undoubtedly had their ups and downs, the founder

(Dan Counsell) isn't a household name, and you've probably never even heard of Clear. But they're out there, still doing their thing, making a living for themselves.

Most Startup Musicians fall under this category. Some of them are featured in this book. They may not be famous, but they're able to get work, pay their bills, and make a living doing music. They may not own a house, and probably don't have millions of dollars in the bank, but that doesn't matter because they're only focused on doing one thing: making great music. This is where I currently find myself. I'm not a rich and famous musician. I'm a guy who plays music for a living. It's amazing.

This is the third option for your startup: keep going, keep making good work, and make a living. It's not glamorous, you won't get rich, and you probably won't be famous, but you get to make good music and make a living doing something you love.

Go Public

For tech startups, this is the dream. Well, kind of like the long-shot dream, or a dream within a dream. In order for a tech startup to achieve this, it must transform itself into a company that can be publicly traded on the stock market.

Facebook went public on May 18, 2012, and opened for trading on the NASDAQ with a valuation of $104 billion. As of my writing in 2017, Facebook just hit a total valuation of $500 billion[26]. Since launching in 2004, Facebook has grown, changed, and evolved to become the (love it or hate it) social media giant that it is today.

This is the ideal scenario for tech startups, but the

---

[26] Matt Egan. "Facebook and Amazon hit $500 billion milestone" CNN Money. (July 27, 2017).

hardest to achieve. If there are *thousands* of startups that fizzle out, there are even more that don't make it being a publicly traded company.

For a Startup Musician, "going public" means that you have solidified yourself as an excellent musician, a pleasure to work with, and worth hiring because you're "you". In this analogy, going public means bursting through those three questions, crossing the threshold, and becoming an established musician. You still probably won't be as famous as Bono (although even *he* was a Startup Musician once upon a time), but you're able to make a living as a musician and live the life that you want.

Zach Rudulph has gone public. He's an essential part of Andy Grammer's team, and even if that operation ends tomorrow, Zach is so good at what he does and so great to work with, he'll be snatched up by another artist in no time. He's established himself as an incredibly valuable musician. When people hire Zach, it's not just because they want a bass player or a music director; they want ZACH RUDULPH.

This is the dream of many Startup Musicians, to transition from startup operation to established musician, one who is valuable not only for what you can do, but also for who you are.

Defining Your Own Success

The way I see it, you've got all four options ahead of you, and while your initial reaction may be "I want option 4!" let me say this: all of the options listed above are valid destinations for a Startup Musician.

Most musicians will try their hand at freelance work and ultimately decide it's not for them. Maybe it's the money, maybe it's the unpredictability, but something will push them toward a more traditional job. No problem. It's completely okay to say, "This is not for me."

Some musicians will marry someone with a stable income (hopefully for love, not for the money). This can help smooth out the finances and a little extra funding can help a startup succeed.

Then there's the musicians who continue to press on, ride the roller coaster of freelance life, and can't imagine doing anything else. The unpredictability is tolerable because *you do music for a living* and that's amazing.

And for the lucky few who go public, you'll establish yourself as a brand, an irreplaceable asset to whatever project you work on. You'll be the type of person that other musicians look up to, seek out for advice, and follow on Instagram because you're…YOU.

With four destinations ahead of you, how will you decide which is right for you? How will you know when you've "made it?" How will you define your own success?

As a Startup Musician, you can have whatever kind of life you want. In this book you've heard from musicians who rent an apartment, rent a house, and own a house. They are single, dating, divorced, and married. Some have kids, or no kids, or a very large tortoise. You've heard from a guitarist, a bassist, a drummer, a keyboard player, a trombone player, a singer, a mastering studio project manager, a teacher, a composer, and a guy producing records out of his home studio.

There's no one right way to do this. It's a path you have to forge yourself. Going forward without a clear roadmap might be frustrating, but it's also an incredible opportunity. You get to make your own path. You get to experiment, try new things, play with lots of people, play different styles, fail spectacularly, and constantly get up, all while doing something you love.

You'll try new things and move on to other things. You'll play plenty of terrible gigs. But eventually, you'll figure out what you're the best at and what part of your startup people value most. You'll do that for a while, and then things will change again. You'll adapt to change with it. You may never have a "This is it! I'm doing it!" moment and there will be a whole lot of "Am I doing it? I guess I'm doing it?" moments, followed by even more "This is it for me, I think my career is over." moments. But then you'll get a call for a gig on Saturday night and it'll all be okay.

In order to make it through these ups and downs, you need to do one crucially important thing. You need to define what "success" means to you. Not to the industry, not to your friends and family, to you.

If you don't define success, you'll spend the rest of your life wondering, "Am I doing it? Am I a successful musician? Is this what I wanted?"

If you don't define success, you'll end up chasing stats and milestones that matter to other people but aren't actually that important to you.

If you don't define success, you'll go through your career comparing yourself to the person next to you and always coming up short.

If you don't define success, you'll go through your career feeling like you're running on a treadmill; exhausted, uninspired, and going nowhere.

Take some time to think specifically about what "success" would look like in your music career.

Where are some places you'd like to play or projects you'd like to work on?

Who are some people you'd like to work with?

What kinds of musical things do you like to do?

What kind of life do you want to have?

How does your career as a Startup Musician fit into that life?

By answering these questions, you'll have a clearer picture of where you're heading and a better idea of when you've "made it."

CHAPTER 23
THE CHEAT SHEET

SparkNotes got me through high school (I still haven't even opened *To Kill a Mockingbird*), so in honor of the greatest way to read without reading, here's the cheat sheet version of this book.

How To Be a Successful Startup Musician: A 17-Step Guide

- Be good at music.
- Choose a few things to focus on and get really world class at those things.
- Get gear that is good enough.
- Make a website and use social media.
- Don't quit your day job yet, and don't be ashamed about that.
- Be your own great boss.
- Remember the 2/3 rule.
- Remember the 0/3 rule.
- Think creatively.
- If you want more work, make more friends. (Network!)

- Focus on the work.
- Keep your musical curiosity.
- Get above the threshold and claim your territory.
- Know that you'll never quite feel like you've made it, and you'll always have doubts.
- Do a free gig every now and then.
- Remember you are more than your music career.
- Live whatever kind of life you want to live.

17 points? I know, that's still a lot. I'm trying here. Tell you what; if I had to boil down everything in this book to just one sentence it's this:

If you want a successful career as a professional musician, be a world class musician and a world class person.

Everything else will fall into place. Everything. If you're a musician who's really great at a few things, you'll be on people's lists for those things. If you're a great person to be around and work with, you'll be even higher on that list.

You don't have to be able to do everything. You don't have to live in downtown LA. You don't have to have the most expensive gear. You don't have be "the best" guitarist, or drummer, or composer, or whatever your thing is. And you don't need to go on The Voice.

You just need to be a great musician and a great person.

Remember the 2/3 rule? There are three factors (money, music, people), and if two of them are good, you take the gig. By being a great musician and a great person, you're already fulfilling 2/3 of the equation (music + people). Hiring you is a no-brainer. That's how Zach Rudulph makes a living playing with Andy Grammer, how Vanessa Bryan makes a living singing and teaching, and how all the other musicians in this book make a living. That's also how I found the 10 musicians to interview for this book.

How did I connect with each of them? Easy. They are all great musicians and they're all friends of mine. We've worked together at some point, and because each one is a great musician and a great person to be around, they're making a living. All I had to do was send a text.

By self-fulfilling the 2/3 rule you move yourself up the call list for all of your friends, and because musicians love working with their friends, you get more work. The more friends you have, the more work you have, and it snowballs from there. But it all starts with being a great musician and a great person.

Yes, I'm oversimplifying, but it's true. When in doubt, ask yourself, "What would the most awesome musician do? What would the most awesome person do?"

I made some handy WWMAMD and WWMAPD bracelets to help you remember. Available for sale at thisisnotarealthing.com.

You'll be surprised how these simple questions can shape your career.

So, get going!

- Go hang out with some musicians that you know. Go to lunch, grab a drink, or play some music together. Just go be a good friend to someone.

- Get plugged in to your local music scene. Go see some live music and introduce yourself after the show. Sit in at a jam session. The musicians in your city are your network, your coworkers. Get to know them.

- Figure out your niche (because I *know* you didn't do it during the first read through) and jot down what gear you have and what gear you need to get. Remember: good enough.

- Make a website to promote your work. Squarespace is easy. Wordpress self hosted is great too. If you go the Wordpress route, check out my free tutorial at www.startupmusician.co/website.

- Figure out what your Work is (again, I know you didn't fill that out the first time), and start doing it. Every. Single. Day.

- Head over to www.startupmusician.co where there are a lot of other resources for professional musicians. I've got articles, podcast interviews, videos, and other free stuff to help you out.

- When you've finished all of that, shoot me an email at brandon@startupmusician.co. I would LOVE to hear from you, the startup you're building, and what you thought of this book. I promise I'll write you back.

• Keep going.

If you are a good musician doing musical things that you enjoy and a good person, you're already successful. It doesn't matter if you're the bass player for Coldplay or not. If you're a professional musician and you like your life, you are a success. You are a Startup Musician.

#startupmusician

ACKNOWLE-DGEMENTS

The creation of this book has been a long journey and I have a lot people to thank. If you're the type of person who stays til the end of the credits because you think there's going to be a bonus scene, I'm sorry to tell you, this isn't a Marvel book. There's no Samuel L. Jackson to be found here. Just lots of sincere thank you's to some wonderful people.

First off, my wife Faith. Thank you for being such a wonderful person, for loving me, encouraging me, and for asking me to play bass with you (finally). I thought once we were married that I'd have this gig on LOCK, and I *do*, but it turns out it works differently than I thought (mainly, you don't pay me anymore). Thank you for supporting me, loving me, encouraging me, and for saying yes to my crazy ideas. You're a wonderful person, musician, singer, songwriter, and I love getting to make music with you. (If you, dear reader, haven't heard her music, please go search for "Faith Shaw" and "Hello Dear" to hear some heartfelt folksy tunes. You'll thank me later.)

A big thank you to Allison Shaw for being an incredible editor. You made this book so much better! It was a joy getting to work with you on it!

Thank you to Prezleigh Moy for transcribing these audio interviews into words. You were the best intern I ever had.

Thank you to Ace Barro for making an amazing book cover, and taking all the photos of me in this book.

Thank you to my my Mom for putting up with me for years, not letting me quit music no matter how many times I insisted I was done because I wasn't catching the G#s. You are the reason I finished college (twice!) and if it weren't for you I probably wouldn't be playing music professionally now. You are the best Mother and best accompanist I've ever had.

Thank you to my Dad for the years of support, talking us to the live recording of Five O' Clock People, buying me a MIDI keyboard, and surprising me with that Fender P Bass that I still play. Your writing and storytelling have inspired me to start a blog, make videos, and write a book and stuff and junk.

Thank you to every teacher I ever had: Mr. Baldock, Mrs. Halstead, Mr. Couch, Mr. C, Mr. Nelson, Brian Johnson, Larry Zgonc, Francis Senger, Tim Emmons, Tim Eckert, and Kristin Korb.

Thank you to Dale Mar for loaning me a bass and amp at age 10. All I ever wanted to do was play your bass line on "You Are Mighty" and when you taught it to me I felt like I was unstoppable. Rest in Peace.

Thank you to David Beatty and Tim Jacquette. I don't remember which one of you gave me the 2/3 analogy (maybe it was both of you), but it obviously stuck with me.

Thank you to Nate Lotz for encouraging me to join Pop Rock. 90% of my work now can be traced back directly to that class.

Thank you to all of my musician friends who have read my blog, listened to the podcast, watched videos, and actually shared it online! You are the reason that I was able to keep going. Thank you all for your support, you know who you are.

Thank you to my brother Ryan for still refusing to take down the Kraft Mac n' Cheese video from YouTube. And for proving me wrong. When you're writing how-to non-fiction, they say instead of trying to write to everyone, focus on writing to one person. That person has always been you (not that you needed my help, clearly).

Thank you to my other brother Kendon for claiming the guitar and leaving me with no other option than to play the bass. If you hadn't, I probably would have ended up a guitarist, and well, I can't think of anything worse.

Lastly, thank YOU, dear reader for buying this book and actually reading it. I can't tell you how much it means to write something, have it printed, and have someone actually read it. And thank you for reading to the end of the thank you's! I truly wish you the best of luck in all your musical pursuits and hope you've enjoyed reading this book as much as I've enjoyed writing it.

ABOUT THE AUTHOR

Photo: Ace Barro (like every other photo of me in this book)

I'm a freelance musician. A Startup Musician, if you will. I play upright, electric, and synth bass. I'm also a Music Director and do everything that goes along with that (see Zach Rudulph's chapter). I also DJ. I also write. I get to play a lot of different music with lots of different people. It's pretty great.

Some people I've played with include Loa Greyson, Tommy Walker, Ethan Bortnick, Crystal Lewis, Teryn Ré Big Band, Quadron, The Angeles Chorale, Jacq Becker, Ry Bradley, Downbeat LA, Faith Shaw, Scott Ryan, Soultones, Jen Oikawa Trio, Sara Pumphrey, and The Los Angeles Collaboration.

You've probably never heard of most of those, right? Perfect. I'm someone who isn't a household name, but gets the incredible privilege of making music for a living.

I've been very fortunate to play music in Italy, Germany, South Korea, Austria, Canada, Switzerland, Russia and all over the United States. Ooh, and I was on PBS. Ooh and KCRW here in LA.

I teach private lessons individually and as an adjunct teacher at Citrus College. I've also taught at multiple summer music camps, and have run camps with some other excellent musicians.

Besides freelancing, teaching, and Startup Musician, I also get to make music with my wonderful wife who is a singer-songwriter.

.

Made in the USA
San Bernardino, CA
23 July 2019